W9-BVS-635

ORTHO'S All About

Masonry
Basics

```
          693.1 Masonry      c.1
Ortho Books.
Ortho's all about masonry basics.
```

Meredith® Books
Des Moines, Iowa

PROPERTY OF
HIGH POINT PUBLIC LIBRARY
HIGH POINT, NORTH CAROLINA

Ortho® Books
An imprint of Meredith® Books

Ortho's All About Masonry Basics
Editor: Larry Erickson
Contributing Editors: Martin Miller, Marilyn Rogers
Art Director: Tom Wegner
Copy Chief: Catherine Hamrick
Copy and Production Editor: Terri Fredrickson
Technical Reviewer: Raymond L. Kast
Contributing Proofreaders: Steve Hallam, Colleen Johnson,
   Ralph Selzer, Debra Morris Smith, Margaret Smith
Contributing Illustrator: Tony Davis
Indexer: Nan Badgett
Electronic Production Coordinator: Paula Forest
Editorial and Design Assistants: Kathleen Stevens,
   Karen Schirm
Contributing Editorial Assistant: Janet Anderson
Production Director: Douglas M. Johnston
Book Production Managers: Pam Kvitne,
   Marjorie J. Schenkelberg

**Additional Editorial Contributions from
   Greenleaf Publishing**
Publishing Director: Dave Toht
Associate Editor: Steve Cory
Assistant Editor: Rebecca JonMichaels
Editorial Art Director: Jean DeVaty
Design: Melanie Lawson Design
Additional Photography: Dan Stultz
Technical Consultant: Michael Clark

Meredith® Books
Editor in Chief: James D. Blume
Design Director: Matt Strelecki
Managing Editor: Gregory H. Kayko

Director, Sales & Marketing, Retail: Michael A. Peterson
Director, Sales & Marketing, Special Markets:
   Rita McMullen
Director, Sales & Marketing, Home & Garden Center
   Channel: Ray Wolf
Director, Operations: George A. Susral

Vice President, General Manager: Jamie L. Martin

Meredith Publishing Group
President, Publishing Group: Christopher M. Little
Vice President, Consumer Marketing & Development:
   Hal Oringer

Meredith Corporation
Chairman and Chief Executive Officer: William T. Kerr

Chairman of the Executive Committee: E.T. Meredith III

Photographers
(Photographers credited may retain copyright ©
   to the listed photographs.)
Pat Bruno: 18-19
David Goldberg: 70 (BR)
John North Holtorf: Cover
Paul Kestner: 9 (BL)
Portland Cement Association: 22 (top)
Ken Rice: 14, 57
Dan Stultz: 6-7, 8, 9 (right), 16 (CL), 22 (bottom), 36
   (top), 50 (TR), 64 (TL), 77, 78, 80-81 (center), 84, 85
   (bottom), 86 (TR), 89 (BL)
US Heritage: 81 (CR), 90 (TR)

All of us at Ortho® Books are dedicated to providing you
with the information and ideas you need to enhance your
home and garden. We welcome your comments and
suggestions about this book. Write to us at:
   Meredith Corporation
   Ortho Books
   1716 Locust St.
   Des Moines, IA 50309–3023

If you would like more information on other Ortho
products, call 800-225-2883 or visit us at www.ortho.com

Copyright © 2000 The Scotts Company
Some text, photography, and artwork copyright © 2000
   Meredith Corporation
All rights reserved. Printed in the United States of America.
First Edition. Printing Number and Year:
   5 4 3 2 1 04 03 02 01 00
Library of Congress Catalog Card Number: 99-75930
ISBN: 0-89721-438-2

Note to the Readers: Due to differing conditions, tools,
and individual skills, Meredith Corporation assumes no
responsibility for any damages, injuries suffered, or losses
incurred as a result of following the information published
in this book. Before beginning any project, review the
instructions carefully, and if any doubts or questions remain,
consult local experts or authorities. Because codes and
regulations vary greatly, you always should check with
authorities to ensure that your project complies with all
applicable local codes and regulations. Always read and
observe all of the safety precautions provided by
manufacturers of any tools, equipment, or supplies,
and follow all accepted safety procedures.

693.1
MASONRY

PLANNING & DESIGN

Masonry projects add elegance and long-lasting beauty to a home. Even a modest brick or paver patio, a backyard stone wall, or a concrete walk can bring charm to your landscape and enhance its usefulness. It's true, masonry projects are hard work, and the results—good or bad—are permanent. Once you finish a project, though, you'll look at it with a sense of pride and accomplishment.

You may feel as though masonry projects are too daunting to tackle. But if you can build a deck or fence, many projects using brick, stone, or concrete are within your current capabilities. With careful planning and after learning a few basic techniques, you can take on more complex tasks.

A do-it-yourselfer who's willing to pitch in and do some hard work can accomplish most of the projects in this book with professional-looking results. Some projects, however, require special skills that cannot be learned quickly. Read the instructions thoroughly, and identify the operations you may have problems accomplishing. Either practice with scrap materials until you feel comfortable, or hire a pro to help with at least part of the job. If done incorrectly, many masonry projects are difficult to redo.

Before you start work, develop an overall landscape plan. This first chapter gets you started. The permanence of masonry work is a compelling reason to think through your design so that the project integrates well into your yard. Careful planning adds to your confidence and can be an enjoyable process for the whole family.

Subsequent chapters in this book lead you through basic masonry projects that can lend a solid grace to your yard: concrete work; patios made of bricks, pavers, or stones; and walls for the garden or for your house. The last chapter tackles the most common masonry repairs.

WORKING TO CODE

Like it or not, there is a government department whose job is to oversee construction in your area. Local communities establish building codes to ensure the safety of residents and to provide standards for consistent quality. Some departments want to inspect any project you do; others don't want to bother with homeowners working in their own backyards. In most communities, though, the codes apply to all permanent structures involving masonry work.

Go to your building department and ask the staff for general information on masonry; they may have literature that explains much of what you need to know. At this point, you may find that your project does not require inspection.

If your project does need to be inspected, draw up a neat and accurate plan (*see page 13*) and present it to the inspector. Don't ask an inspector what to do; his or her job is to inspect, not to advise.

Once a plan is approved, you'll need to schedule one or more inspections. Be clear as to what you should have done—and what should not be done—when the inspector arrives. A common mistake is to push a project along, covering up what the inspector needs to see. Keep in mind that cooperating with the inspector and working to code are in your best interest.

Planning a masonry project needn't be confined to linear thinking. Though complex to lay out and execute, undulating curves are possible in masonry projects.

BRICKS AND PAVERS

Bricks come in many sizes, colors, and textures, and each variation has specific uses. The heat of the kiln and the local clay mix give brick its unique color. Texture is determined by how the brick is cut or molded. Most smooth-surfaced bricks are made by the water-struck process. Sand-struck brick has a sandpapery surface; wire-cut brick is rough.

TYPES OF BRICK

BUILDING BRICK, also called common or standard brick, is generally imperfect in appearance, and it is often chipped. The blemishes add to its rustic charm, which transfers to the finished project.

For structures subject to moisture and freezing, use SW-grade (severe-weather) bricks. Where bricks won't be permeated with water in freezing weather, MW (moderate-weather) bricks will do. No-weathering, grade-NW, bricks are suitable for indoor projects only.

FACING BRICK usually has a nicely finished surface. In projects where there are several wythes (a wythe is a one-brick-thick vertical section of masonry), the interior wythes are usually made of common building brick and the exterior is facing brick. FBX facing bricks are nearly perfect; FBS bricks have some variation in color and surface; FBA units are used for variety in color and texture and for architectural effects.

Common and facing brick may be solid, have holes (called cored brick), or have an indentation (called a frog). The holes and indentations help lock bricks in mortar. Lay brick so that the frogs are face down in the mortar. Use solid bricks for walks, patios, and caps of walls. Use cored bricks in places where the holes will not be visible, such as in a wall or planter box.

FIREBRICK, easily identified by its yellow color, is made with a special clay and fired at extremely high temperatures. It is used as a lining for fireplaces or barbecues because of its heat-resistant qualities. Firebrick requires a special refractory cement or fireclay mortar that won't fall apart under high temperatures.

PAVING BRICK is harder than common brick and is used for brick-in-sand and mortared patios and driveways. Paving brick is classified according to how much traffic load it can bear and its ability to resist weathering. Use type 3 or type 2 for maximum load capacity; use class SX for harsh wet winters, MS for exterior use in mild climates, and NX for interior work.

3-hole common brick

Manufactured "used" brick

Brick with "frog" indentation

10-hole

3-hole

Rough facing brick

Bay corner facing brick for a bay window

Wire-cut facing brick

Firebrick

PAVERS are not true bricks, because they are made of concrete, but they're used like paving brick. More durable than brick and less expensive, pavers come in many shapes, sizes, textures, and colors. They offer a cost-effective, attractive alternative to brick for walks, driveways, patios, and walls. Some manufacturers design their pavers to interlock, assuring a solid surface.

SALVAGED BRICKS have a warm and rustic charm but may be expensive and not as weather resistant as new brick. Inspect them for quality, particularly if they are 30 or more years old. Modern bricks use better clays and improved firing techniques. An alternative is manufactured "used" bricks—building or concrete bricks with gray and white splotches that make them look worn.

GLAZED BRICKS are face bricks treated with liquid glazing before being fired in the kiln. The result is a glassy surface. This kind of brick works nicely in kitchens and bathrooms because it is easy to clean.

CLINKER BRICKS are rough, hard, and often dark or deformed as a result of the high heat in the kiln. They are usually used for decorative purposes.

SIZE, COLOR, AND TEXTURE

SIZE: Like lumber, bricks are referred to by their nominal dimensions rather than exact sizes, to account for the width of mortar joints—usually ³⁄₈ inch. For example, a 4×8-inch brick is actually 3⁵⁄₈ inches wide and 7⁵⁄₈ inches long. Unless you are doing precise work, you don't have to worry about this difference.

Bricks come in modular sizes, meaning they are sized in increments of 4 inches. This means that one brick fits across two side-by-side bricks, making it simpler to fit walls and patios together.

COLOR: Virtually all brick colors are in the warm range of color—red, brown, and yellow—but the variations can be significant. Except for high-quality facing brick, most brick is not uniform in color. For example, flashed brick has light and dark scorch marks. These color irregularities add to the charm of brick in the landscape.

TEXTURE: In addition to the many colors available, bricks come in different textures. Among the common textures are smooth face, stippled face, and matte face. A fingerprint brick has indentations that look as if they were made by a thumb. When considering bricks for a patio or sidewalk, choose a texture that will provide a nonslip walking surface.

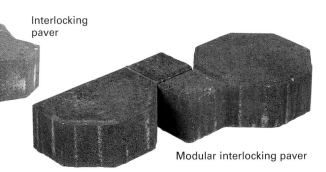

Interlocking paver

Modular interlocking paver

Shaped concrete pavers work as an ensemble to form a circular pattern.

Flashed brick

Salvaged brick

Fingerprint brick

Speckled brick

Pigmented brick

Multicolored ace facing brick

BLOCK AND STONE

If you want to build a masonry wall in a hurry, and if appearance is not a priority, concrete block is the way to go. To bring out the best in a woodland setting, though, nothing works like natural stone. Both materials are heavy, so use caution if you're not used to lifting them.

CONCRETE BLOCK

Concrete block has two or three hollow spaces, called cells, with dividers, called webs, at each end. Don't confuse it with "cinder block," which is not as strong.

Walls built of standard concrete block must be mortared in place, and they require footings. You may opt instead to use interlocking blocks, some of which do not require footings or mortar. Simply lay this block directly on gravel in a shallow trench (*see page 71*). You can also stack the blocks dry (*see photo on page 70*), then apply a stuccolike surface bond.

Concrete block comes in several forms:

STANDARD BLOCK is about 8 inches wide, 8 inches high, and 16 inches long. Actual dimensions are ⅜ inch less,

6×8×16
wall block

4×8×16 block

for the mortar joint. Block widths of 4, 6, 10, and 12 inches are also available, as is 8-inch-square block, called half block. Half block is commonly used at the ends of walls, which allows you to stagger the joints.

STRETCHER BLOCK has ribs at each end, which you "butter" with mortar then join.

CORNER BLOCK has a ribbed end for butting to the adjacent block, and a smooth end that is exposed.

DECORATIVE BLOCK is available in several styles. Curved-end block adds a decorative touch at the end of a wall. Blocks with split faces look like hand-hewn stone. There are also blocks with sculptured faces, and slump block, which closely resembles adobe brick. Plain concrete blocks look drab; but stuccoing them creates a wall that is warm and pleasing (*see pages 70 and 78–79*).

NATURAL STONE

The natural good looks of stone go well with almost any landscape and house, and building a stone wall does not require the skill needed for a brick or block wall. Most stone used in masonry projects comes from quarries or is found in open areas. Quarried stone includes marble, flagstone, and slate. It can be dressed (cut and trimmed to set sizes) or semidressed (rough-cut stone). Ashlar is cut precisely; the pieces fit together in a pattern.

Fieldstone, found in fields, woods, and along rivers and streams, is divided into two classes—rubble and squared. Rubble is

U block for
over lintels

Block with
decorative face

Rounded
half corner

Basic stretcher

Curved
block for
retaining wall

Half corner
block

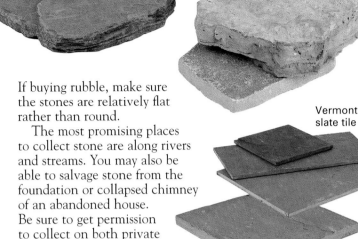

Rough slate

Flagstone

unworked stone in its natural state. Squared stone has been roughly worked over with a hammer and chisel to facilitate fitting one stone against another. Cut-face stone has a fairly smooth face but fits together in a random manner, like rubble.

Worked stone is best for walkways and patios. Among your choices are:

FLAGSTONE is typically formed from limestone or sandstone. It is a cut stone in flat, square or irregularly shaped, 2- to 4-inch-thick pieces. Use thin pieces for patio surfaces (*see pages 52–53*) and thick pieces for garden walls or flower beds. A flagstone patio is beautiful but may be too uneven for walking or scooting furniture around on.

SLATE is available in irregularly shaped, 2-inch-thick pieces. Depending on the quarry your supplier buys from, it may have a green or purple hue or be gray or black. For indoor use or for a smooth mortared patio, buy slate labeled "Vermont tile."

STONE TILE is cut as precisely as standard tile and available in nearly any type of stone, stone tile is installed in the same manner as standard tile, with mortar and spacers.

WHERE TO FIND STONE

You can buy stone or collect it yourself. If you buy it, compare the stones, prices, and delivery costs of several sources. Squared stone is the most expensive; semidressed stone costs less but is more expensive than rubble.

Ashlar

Rubble (unworked, natural stone)

Cut-face natural stone

If buying rubble, make sure the stones are relatively flat rather than round.

The most promising places to collect stone are along rivers and streams. You may also be able to salvage stone from the foundation or collapsed chimney of an abandoned house. Be sure to get permission to collect on both private and public property. (**Caution!** *Fieldstone often shelters bees or snakes. Always lift the stone with a long pry bar to allow whatever may be lurking to escape. See the lifting techniques on page 15.*)

Vermont slate tile

Slate tile

Stone tile

LOOSE STONE

For patios or paths that receive little traffic, you may opt for the easiest masonry installation of all: Merely excavate the path a few inches; line the path with landscape fabric to keep weeds out; install edging, such as 4×4 lumber; then pour in loose stone and tamp it firmly. Small-gauge stone is surprisingly stable.

Many suppliers offer bins of stone to choose from. Quartz pebbles, crushed granite, and red lava rock make good firm surfaces, though not for walking barefoot. River rock—large, smooth pebbles—is striking in appearance but doesn't compact well, making it most useful as decoration.

River rock

Crushed granite

Red lava rock

ADOBE

Traditional adobe is a southwestern material made of clay and straw, and little else, and is unsuitable for use in wet or cold climates. Asphalt-reinforced adobe, however, is usable in most climates, and makes an excellent patio or short garden wall. Its soft appearance lends charm to landscaping, even in cold, damp northern settings.

LANDSCAPE DESIGN

Successful masonry projects grow out of careful design that integrates the features of your yard and house with the outdoor needs of your family. When planning a new structure for your yard, balance your current specific needs with the big picture. Consider the strong points as well as the disadvantages of your site—its size, contours, drainage patterns, major plants, sun exposure, wind direction, and garden structures. Use masonry projects to solve problems such as lack of privacy.

Be sure that any new structure does not detract from the existing features of your landscape. For example, in the wrong spot, even the most handsome garden wall can block the view from your kitchen window. Or a patio might take over space that's now devoted to a lovely flower garden.

This brick walk combines two patterns. Its rectangular form both frames the backyard herb garden and provides for easy harvesting.

GETTING STARTED

Start by deciding how you want to use your landscape. Then focus on the design and shape of the structures. A key element of good landscaping is consistent style. Consulting a landscape designer or doing your own research will help make your landscape project pleasing and attractive. Visiting nurseries and garden shops, consulting a university extension center, or studying yards and gardens that you like—all are inexpensive ways to do research.

Walls, walkways, patios, decks, and other permanent structures are referred to as "hardscape." Plantings are called "softscape." As you design your landscape, choose structures and plantings that complement each other as well as the overall design.

Look for materials that are compatible with your surroundings. Your landscape should blend in with your home's architectural style, the predominant landscaping materials and features of your neighborhood, and the native landscape. For example, a fence would look out of place in a neighborhood of open yards; desert plantings suit the Southwest but may be difficult to integrate into a wooded lot. The better you understand your surroundings, the more skillfully your project will blend in with unique and distinctive effects.

This stone wall is a beautiful foil for the natural wood and foliage of an informal garden.

DESIGN PRINCIPLES

The basic principles of design are universal, no matter what the specific features or constraints of your landscape. If you are forging your own design, use the following principles to organize and focus your ideas.

VIEWS AND PERSPECTIVE: Perspective is the appearance of an object from a vantage point. When designing your landscape, look at it from different places. Sit under a large shade tree at the end of the yard and look across the yard at the house. This is one perspective. Take another look, this time from a second-story window. This perspective may give you a different impression. Devise a plan that looks good from many angles.

COLOR: A little bit of this powerful element goes a long way. For example, a few pots of bright red flowers draw the eye, but they also change the viewer's perspective.

Color can modify depth perception: Pale plantings or surfaces create a feeling of spaciousness, whereas dark ones help define boundaries. Dark red masonry naturally complements green foliage; so does pink, but pink calls more attention to itself. Neutral tones, like tan and gray, are excellent background colors, while white and dark colors create stark contrast. Any color that's used too much becomes monotonous.

PROPORTION: Patios and walls should neither overwhelm the house nor look puny beside it. Architects often use a rule of thumb to create pleasing balance: For every 7 feet of wall against which the patio abuts, make the patio 5 feet long. For example, a house that is 28 feet long calls for a 20-foot-long patio. A slightly smaller patio would be acceptable, but a much larger one would seem out of proportion. There's no such formula for walls and their relationship to houses, but the principle remains the same. A massive garden wall will dwarf a small house, while a small, stone, 2-foot-high raised flower bed will seem out of place next to a large house.

THEME AND VARIATION: Resist any temptation to throw too many different designs and shapes into your landscaping.

Simplicity is often the hallmark of the best designs. Bring a pleasant sense of unity-with-diversity to your yard by using a feature, such as a shape or a distinctive building material, in various places throughout the landscape. For example, repeat a certain curve or angle from the patio in a wall or other structure. Or the same limestone that edges a flower bed could be used in smaller structures here and there. Avoid obvious repetition; the final effect should be subtle.

Select masonry to complement your setting. A formal home (top) benefits from varied flagstones. Square pavers (bottom) contrast pleasingly with a lakeside setting.

DRAWING A PLAN

Gathering ideas is the first step in landscape design: Clip pictures from magazines, jot down notes, and take photos while on neighborhood walks. Keep these in a file for easy reference.

MAKE A BASE PLAN

A base plan is a detailed map of the entire site that you plan to landscape, drawn to scale. You'll need graph paper (large sheets work best), tracing paper, a ⅛-inch-scale or architect's ruler, pencils, erasers, and a long tape measure (preferably 100 feet).

If you have a property survey (a plat), you can use its measurements for your plan. If not, or to ensure accuracy, measure the perimeter of your property and the distance from the sides of your house to the property line. Then accurately draw your property lines and house on graph paper, using a scale of ⅛ inch = 1 foot (¼ inch = 1 foot on larger graph paper). Orient your drawing so the top of the paper represents north.

Next, measure significant landscape features and add them to the drawing. These include the doors and windows of the house (for determining views and perspective); the location of exterior faucets and electrical outlets; tree outlines; driveways and paths; and the location of underground utilities.

Now draw in any landscaping features that affect the way you use your yard—sloped areas, changes in soil type, and other natural features. Show the street and any significant features on adjacent properties, such as trees or buildings that shade your yard. Indicate the direction of prevailing winds, the location of sunny or shaded areas, and low spots that collect water. Daily sun and shade patterns are particularly important. Be aware of patterns for the months of the year when you will be using outdoor areas. Note points of access and patterns of movement—doors, gates, and paths—including foot traffic across lawns and other open areas.

MAKE BUBBLE PLANS

With the base plan drawn, your family can then record and revise their ideas for using the yard on a "bubble" plan (*left*). Tape a piece of tracing paper over your base plan, or make several full-sized copies of it at a copy center. Hang the tracing paper-covered plan or one of the copies where everyone in the family can access it, such as on the kitchen wall or on the refrigerator. Then make a list of all the ways your family would like to use the yard. Draw circles—bubbles—on the plan to indicate locations for those uses. Encourage all family members to add, scratch out, and change ideas.

You may, for instance, want to position a hammock or lounge chair in a spot that has dappled sunlight and a pleasant view. Or it may make more sense to put it in a spot where you can keep an eye on the kids as you relax. Dining and barbecuing areas should have easy access to the kitchen. Wide steps can provide overflow seating during parties.

As a copy becomes cluttered, transfer the best ideas to a clean copy of the base plan. Then let family members further refine their ideas. Don't be afraid to revise your plan many times. The children may want a play area

BASE AND BUBBLE PLANS

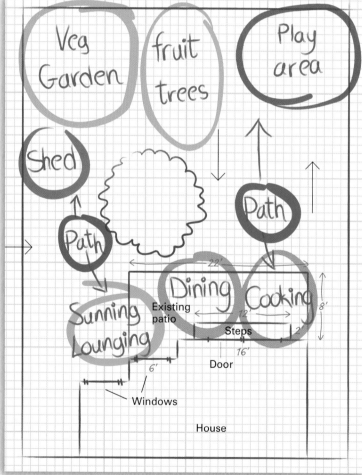

The first stage in developing your landscape plan is to make a carefully drawn base plan. Then you create bubble plans, loosely sketched ideas for using the yard, on a copy of the base plan. Each bubble shows where an activity will take place. Here, the vegetable garden is positioned to catch the sun in a southern exposure, and the play area is readily visible from the house. The patio will accommodate lounging, dining, and cooking.

MINIMUM SIZES FOR OUTDOOR USE AREAS

The best way to choose a size for your dining area is to set your table and chairs on the lawn and measure. But for planning purposes, start with these general guidelines. The dimensions below are minimums; making the areas a bit larger will add a feeling of spaciousness.

Dining	12'×12' will provide room for a square or round table with six chairs.
Cooking	5'×8' gives just enough room for a barbecue, a small table, and a few people standing around.
Lounge chair	A 5'×8' space allows ample room for getting in and out of the chair and for setting drinks and snacks nearby.
Walkway	Whether it is an actual path or a part of a patio that will be used as a path, leave a space 4' wide.

where you want flower beds. A proposed bank of trees may shade your garden. Be sure to consider the rapidly changing needs of young children.

To keep the plan from becoming unwieldy, set some ground rules, such as deadlines, agreements to evaluate all suggestions, and an understanding that cost may determine what can be done.

WORKING DRAWINGS

Once you've come up with a final bubble plan, make working drawings (right). Sketch in the details of the elements you've decided to add: decks, patios, walks, raised flower beds, fences, trees, shrubs, and flower beds. Include features such as new electrical outlets and outdoor lighting. Draw everything to scale on a tracing paper overlay, because you'll probably have to change a few things. Besides the plan view, make elevations (side views) and sectionals (cross sections) of any structures you plan to build. These show foundation and construction details.

If the local building department will be inspecting your work, be sure that the working drawings meet their specifications. For concrete work, you'll probably need to show exact thicknesses as well as dimensions of any reinforcing metal. Retaining walls over 3 feet tall will likely require a drainage plan.

GROUND TEST

As a final test to see whether all your plans mesh, do a dry run in the yard. Mark a path with hoses or ropes. Set outdoor furniture on the site of a future patio. Lay stones on the place where you plan to build a flower bed. Test to make sure that everything will be easy to use and not feel cramped.

WORKING DRAWINGS

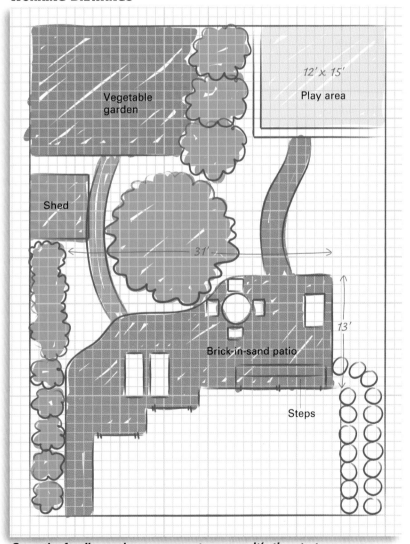

Once the family reaches agreement on uses, it's time to turn your ideas into a working drawing. This is the document you'll work with as you create your new landscape. In this plan, a larger brick-in-sand patio replaces the old concrete slab. Two brick-on-concrete steps lead from the house to the patio. Stepping-stones make a path to the vegetable garden. The kids' play area, reached by a brick-in-sand path, is in view from most of the patio.

PLANNING THE JOB

Unlike interior remodeling, landscape construction projects don't intrude on indoor living space, so it may not matter if an outdoor job takes a month or so. But there are limits: Don't let your yard become a muddy construction site for the greater part of the summer. You may regret ever taking on the project. Here's how to gain a clear idea of the scope of work and your ability to perform it.

SHOULD YOU HIRE A PRO?

Should you do the work yourself? How about doing certain parts yourself and hiring contractors for the rest? Or, should you let pros handle the whole thing? To answer these questions, read about the project carefully. Then assess your skills, your strength, and the amount of volunteer labor you'll need and have available. Hire a pro to do the part you don't feel comfortable with, and do the rest yourself.

If you decide to hire someone to do some or all of the work, ask friends and neighbors for referrals. Drive around town. When you see work that looks good, stop and ask the owner who designed or installed it. Garden centers often recommend landscape architects, designers, and contractors.

Two jobs will likely require some special experience: finishing concrete to a smooth

DO YOU NEED A PERMIT?

Your masonry project, whether it's a driveway, slab, walk, or patio, may require a building permit. Check with your local building department before you begin—codes vary from community to community.

If you do not obtain a permit for work that requires one, you run the risk of a stop-work order and fines. Or the project may be discovered when you try to sell the house, resulting in both fines and delays in closing.

surface, and laying a tall brick wall. Even a skilled contractor may have trouble producing a smooth concrete surface or laying a wall that looks straight.

CHOOSING A CONTRACTOR: Get bids from at least three contractors. Your drawings and descriptions of work will ensure that all prospective contractors are bidding on the same work. Your plans need not be professional-quality, but they should be detailed enough to serve as a starting point for discussions. These discussions allow you to see how each contractor refines your ideas.

Before hiring, ask for and check three references. Ask the contractors whether they'll use subcontractors. Visit completed projects as well as job sites with work under

A large concrete job requires serious organizational skills. All the materials need to be on hand, and a crew of workers must work in harmony. If you are planning a large driveway or patio, consider hiring professionals or round up some experienced volunteers.

construction. Ask the owners whether they are satisfied with the work and with the contractor's attitude. Ask for and check bank references. Make sure that the company is financially stable. You could be liable for liens on your property if the contractors do not pay their bills.

PUT IT IN WRITING: A contract must specify who is responsible for performing the work, what work is involved, and at what cost. Most reputable contractors have their own form. It doesn't have to be elaborate, but insist on clarity. Read the contract carefully, and don't hesitate to ask for more detail if something isn't clear. If you have a problem in the future, you and your contractor will use the document to resolve the conflict.

A good contract will include the following, though some of these items may not pertain to your situation:

■ **REFERENCE TO CONSTRUCTION DOCUMENTS:** Your base plan, working drawings, and written description of the work guide the job and become part of the contract. For small jobs, a description of the work and the materials specifications will do.

■ **PAYMENT SCHEDULE:** Payments are usually staggered, with the final payment made *after final inspection.*

■ **CERTIFICATE OF INSURANCE:** The contractor should have both workers' compensation and liability insurance.

■ **STIPULATION OF RESPONSIBILITY:** It is the contractor's responsibility to obtain permits, perform the work to code, and get the necessary inspections. Make sure that startup and completion dates are specified.

When the work is completed, inspected, and approved, make sure that the contractor provides a signed receipt and lien releases before you make final payment. A lien release is a standard form stating that you have paid the contractor for the work. It assures that you won't be held responsible for paying suppliers or subcontractors.

PREPARING FOR CONSTRUCTION

Anything you can do ahead of time to make the job go smoothly is time well spent. First, make sure you have the right tools. Read the description of your project and make a complete tool list. Many tools, such as a brickset or concrete float, are

TAXES AND MASONRY

The type of patio you build could affect your property taxes. Some communities consider a concrete patio to be a permanent improvement and will raise your taxes accordingly. A brick-in-sand patio of the same size may be taxed at a lower rate or not at all.

As part of your planning process, give the local tax assessor a call to see how your project may be taxed. If your job requires a permit, the building department usually sends a copy of the permit application to the local assessor's office, and in some cases, an assessor will inspect the site after building department approval is issued.

inexpensive and are worth buying for only one job. It's better to rent large specialty tools, such as a plate compactor, rebar bender, or cement mixer.

Next, assemble or schedule delivery of all the materials you need for the project. Many are heavy, messy, or bulky, so plan how you will transport and store them. Others, such as expansion-joint material or masking tape, are easy to overlook. Begin a detailed materials list as you read this book.

Finally, prepare yourself for construction. Read through directions completely before beginning. Plan every aspect of the project. And be sure your body is ready to take the beating required, or hire some strong backs to help out.

When lifting heavy stones or repeatedly working with bricks, you can injure your back and not even feel the pain until the next morning. Avoid injury by lifting with your legs, not your back, and use helpers whenever possible.

The right way to lift a stone

The wrong way to lift

LAYING OUT MASONRY PROJECTS

For each batter board, cut a point on two 3-foot-long 2×4s. Drive them into the ground so they are solid. Mark level lines on these legs, then attach the crosspiece with four screws.

No doubt you can't wait to start your project. But you'll thank yourself later if you take time to establish careful layout lines. These provide accurate references for making straight edges, square corners, and level (or evenly sloped) surfaces.

BATTER BOARDS

Start with batter boards. These allow you to take down the layout lines and put them up again throughout the construction process. Before building them, hammer a stake where each corner will be. Connect the stakes with nylon mason's line—it doesn't stretch and sag. As you do so, use a framing square to roughly determine the right angles of each corner.

To check for square, measure the diagonals. In other words, measure the distance between the stakes that are catercorner from each other. If the distances are equal, the area is square. Move stakes until the measurements fall within an inch or two.

Batter boards consist of two 2×4 stakes and one 1×4 crosspiece. First, drive the stakes firmly in the ground at each corner. On a job that you'll dig by hand, set the boards about

For small jobs on a flat surface, use a framing square or an uncut sheet of plywood, as here, to roughly establish square corners.

2 feet apart, 4 feet behind the preliminary corner stakes. If you'll be excavating with a backhoe, set the stakes 10 feet back so the operator can maneuver inside them.

LEVELING

For your wall or patio to be level, the crosspieces must be level with each other. On small jobs, use a mason's line and a line level to make level marks on all the stakes. Align the tops of the crosspieces with the marks, then nail or screw them to the stakes.

Use a water level for large jobs—this is essentially a length of transparent tubing filled with water. It follows the principle that water always seeks its own level.

Fill the tubing with water, then stretch it between the batter boards. Have a helper

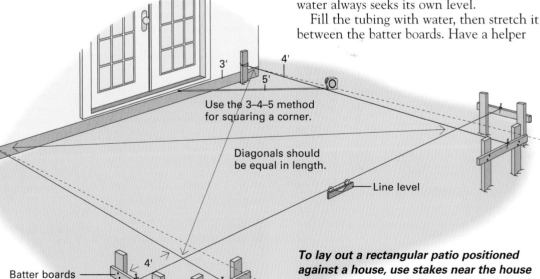

Use the 3–4–5 method for squaring a corner.

Diagonals should be equal in length.

Line level

Batter boards

To lay out a rectangular patio positioned against a house, use stakes near the house and batter boards at the corners. Square the strings perpendicular to the house using the 3-4-5 method. Then measure the sides, set the final string, and check the diagonals.

USING A TRANSIT

Rent a builder's level or a transit for fast and accurate leveling. A transit is a small, tripod-mounted telescope that remains perfectly level no matter which direction you aim it. Set the tripod far enough back from the low corner of the building site that you can see all four corners of the site. Level the instrument with the bubbles on the mounting ring. Work with a helper to make corner lines that are level.

hold one end against each of the stakes and mark where the waterline settles. Then when attaching the crosspieces, line them up with the marks.

STRINGING AND SQUARING

Mark the first side of your layout by stretching mason's line between the batter boards, aligning it over the preliminary corner stakes. Pull the line taut, and tie it to nails driven into the tops of the crosspieces. Attach the other lines in the same way.

The four lines (or three lines and the house) should create a rectangle with square (90-degree) corners. Use the 3–4–5 method to check for square. Mark a point 3 feet from the corner along one string line (or house wall) with a piece of tape. Then mark a point exactly 4 feet from the corner along the intersecting string line. Measure the distance between these points. If it

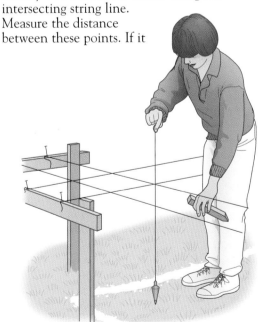

is exactly 5 feet, the corner is a 90-degree angle. If not, readjust the lines until the two markers are 5 feet apart. For large jobs, use multiples of 3, 4, and 5 feet—such as 6, 8, and 10; or 9, 12, and 15.

To double-check for square, measure both diagonals, adjusting the lines until the diagonals are equal and each side is the required length. Finish by cutting notches in the crosspieces, so you can take the lines down and restring them at the same point later.

MARKING THE LAYOUT

Suspend a plumb bob at one corner where string lines intersect. Drive a stake into the ground directly under the plumb bob to mark the corner. Repeat at each corner.

The mason's line is the excavation line. You can leave the line in place or mark its location with flour, sand, chalk, or paint.

If using forms to build a footing for the project, offset the corner stakes and the mason's line to allow for the thickness of the forms (*see pages 26–27*). Inside edges of the form boards must align with the layout lines.

To mark curved edges, use a rope or a "charged" hose—one that is filled with water but shut off at the nozzle; it's firmer than an unfilled hose. Lay the rope or hose in position, then pour flour, sand, or chalk along its length. When you pick up the hose, you'll have a clear excavation line.

Above: With a bag of sand and a hose, you can easily mark tight or gentle curves.

Left: Hold a plumb bob at the intersection of two string lines, then mark the corner by driving a stake in the ground underneath it. When digging a footing, mark its dimensions with mason's line and sand or flour, too.

If possible, set up your site so the mixer truck can back right up to the forms. Then the driver can simply move the chute to pour the concrete where you want it. Most chutes extend 15 feet from the truck. If you can't bring the truck this close without damaging property, have wheelbarrows and plank paths ready (see page 34).

CONCRETE FOUNDATIONS & SLABS

Concrete may not be the most beautiful masonry material, but it is inexpensive and quick to install. It is versatile, too, able to take on almost any shape you choose. This chapter includes techniques for all types and phases of concrete work, from building forms to finishing and curing. You'll find all you need to know to build a patio, walk, stairway, low wall, footing, wall foundation, or slab for a garage.

Concrete is the foundation of many masonry and carpentry projects. Brick walls and mortared stone walls require concrete footings; otherwise, the wall may shift, cracking the mortar. A concrete footing, especially if reinforced with metal, provides a solid basis for an addition or other major structure. When building a deck, shed, or other structure, often the first step is to pour post footings.

Most concrete surfaces are a dull but inoffensive light gray. If that doesn't fit your style, liven things up by adding color, exposing the aggregate, or applying a custom finish (see page 38). You can also use a concrete slab or wall as the substrate for a durable tile or stone surface (see pages 54–56).

The phrase "set in concrete" alerts us to a serious danger: Once it's poured and set, there is little you can do to alter it. Mistakes are usually impossible to correct. And once a slab is poured, you have only a short time to finish it. So this chapter emphasizes getting ready for the pour by having all your forms in place and all the necessary tools on hand. Also, you'll need to get plenty of help—strong backs for moving the concrete around and skilled hands for smoothing the surface.

GETTING JUST ENOUGH HELP

You and your friends may get together on a weekend to build a small deck, replace some siding, or do any number of do-it-yourself projects. Likely, the results will be fine. If mistakes happen, they'll be fixable. But take care when planning concrete work because once poured, a couple hundred square feet of wet concrete can get out of control in a hurry, with miserable results.

If you are unsure of your ability to finish a concrete surface, contact a concrete finisher. Try the yellow pages in the phone book, although most listings there are contractors who want to do the whole job. You could also visit a concrete construction site during lunch, and ask if a finisher would like to take on a small job for a day. Be sure you know how many square feet need to be finished and how smooth you want it to be. Don't expect the pro to do anything but finish, unless you have arranged for more help beforehand. Otherwise, be aware that you're the one who pours and moves the concrete. But be sure to have the finisher on hand before the truck begins pouring.

TOOLS FOR CONCRETE

Pouring and finishing concrete calls for special tools that aren't part of the typical homeowner's collection. So prepare for a tool-buying opportunity.

Most tools for working concrete are uncomplicated and relatively inexpensive; but like all tools, they come in various qualities. Always buy the best-quality you can afford because it's difficult to achieve professional results with cheap tools.

When it comes to power tools, consider renting them. You may even want to rent everything, right down to the trowels, if you're sure you won't be doing another job. But check the price of hand tools before renting—there may not be much difference in cost between renting and buying.

TOOLS FOR REMOVING OLD CONCRETE: Among the tools you should have on hand is a sledge hammer or maul. These can do a surprising amount of damage when you need to demolish old concrete. You can smash slabs that are 3 inches thick or less with a sledge. For thicker concrete, rent a jackhammer. A lightweight electric jackhammer is effective for chopping concrete up to 5 inches thick. For thicker slabs, you'll need a heavy pneumatic jackhammer with a compressor.

FOR REMOVING GRASS: A sod cutter, which uses a roller and a blade to harvest sod, not only makes removing sod easier, but it also produces strips of sod that you can use elsewhere on your property.

DIGGING TOOLS: For excavating the site, a couple of shovels or spades may be all you need. (Technically, on a shovel, the blade is angled for scooping loose material; a spade has a straight blade for digging.)

Pointed or round-point spades work well for removing sod and digging hard ground. A square spade is a must for making neat corners and edges in the soil and for leveling the bottom of an excavation. It doesn't

Electric jackhammer

pay to buy the cheapest shovel or spade. Cheap tools don't keep a sharp edge, and their handles may break when you're prying out rocks or roots.

TAMPING: The earth or gravel base of a project must be firm before you lay concrete. In some cases, you need to tamp the base to firm it. For a small job, a hand tamper does a fairly good job. Buy a ready-made tamper, rent one, or make your own. To make a tamper, nail a 10×10-inch piece of ⅝-inch plywood to the end of a 4×4.

Hand-tamping is hard work, so for larger jobs or where you are concerned that you can't get the substrate firm enough by hand-tamping, rent a vibrating power tamper or a plate compactor.

SMOOTHING AND FINISHING TOOLS: Finishing concrete requires a selection of floats and trowels.

Floats are flat, rectangular, wooden or magnesium tools. You use them to smooth freshly poured concrete mix. An elongated version called a darby extends your reach. It's about 2 feet long. For large jobs, use a bull float, which is 4 to 5 feet long and 8 inches wide and is attached to a long handle.

Magnesium floats are lightweight, so they're easier to work with than wooden floats. They also resist sticking to wet concrete.

Like floats, concrete trowels are flat rectangular tools, but they're usually made of steel. Use them for the last go-over if you want a smooth, slick surface, like that of a garage floor.

At times when the concrete can harden faster than you can work, such as in hot weather or when floating a large slab, consider renting a power finisher-float. The rental clerk can give you instructions for operating it. With a little practice, even a novice can learn to make a fairly smooth surface in short order.

For a nonslip surface, you can finish the concrete with a broom to create grooves. Use a wide, stiff-bristled push broom. The stiffer

Tools for smoothing and finishing freshly poured concrete include trowels and floats. For large jobs, consider renting a power finisher-float.

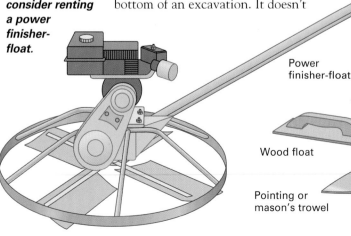

Power finisher-float

Wood float

Steel trowel

Pointing or mason's trowel

RENTING TIPS

If you will be using a tool for one job only and will probably not need it again for several years, rent it. Rental tools may not be shiny and new-looking, but you should find them clean and well maintained. If not, consider going to a different rental shop.

Call several rental outlets, not only to compare costs and availability, but also to get an idea of how helpful the staff is. The staff of a good rental firm should be able to give you complete instructions for operating any tool as well as demonstrate how it works.

Plan carefully to avoid paying for time that the tool is idle: Do all the prep work before picking up the tool at the shop. Be sure to clean rental tools completely before returning them to avoid extra charges.

Circular saw with masonry blade

the bristles, the deeper the grooves will be. (To extend its life, rinse the broom immediately after using it.)
FOR HAULING:
A wheelbarrow is a necessity for concrete work. It handles many jobs: carrying away excavated soil, providing a spot to mix small amounts of concrete, and transporting ready-mixed concrete to spots when the chute can't reach. Be sure the tire is inflated and the handles feel comfortable.

Spade

Shovel

Hand tamper

The trough of the wheelbarrow can be plastic, as long as it is firmly attached to the frame. Buy "contractor-quality" if you want to make sure the wheelbarrow can handle heavy loads. When moving a lot of concrete mix, have at least two wheelbarrows available.
CUTTING: You'll need wire cutters to trim reinforcing mesh. Cutting reinforcing bar—rebar—requires a circular saw with a metal-cutting blade, a reciprocating saw with a metal blade, or a hacksaw. For large projects, there's a tool made especially for cutting and bending rebar, which you can rent. Rebar can be bent by hand (be sure to wear gloves); but if you have a lot to do, rent a rebar bender.
SAFETY TOOLS: Provide rubber gloves for all crew members. On a large slab, at least one person will be sloshing around in the wet concrete, so have a pair of snugly fitting rubber boots ready. (Concrete mix really sticks; it's not uncommon for someone's foot to pull out of a boot.)
SPECIALTY TOOLS: Two other specialized tools you may need are a jointer and an edger. Use the jointer to cut grooves in the concrete to allow for expansion. Edgers are for rounding off edges of the concrete.
MIXERS: In some cases, it makes sense to rent a concrete mixer; but for small amounts, use the wheelbarrow. For larger amounts, have ready-mix delivered.
MISCELLANEOUS: Have on hand several 5-gallon buckets for carrying small amounts of concrete mix and for washing tools. You'll also need some straight 2×4s long enough to span your forms to level the freshly poured concrete. These are called screeds.
FOR HARDENED CONCRETE: Use a heavy-duty circular saw equipped with a masonry blade to cut hardened concrete. To drill holes, a hammer drill works faster than standard models. Have several masonry bits handy if you need to drill a number of holes, because the bits quickly burn out.

Hammer drill

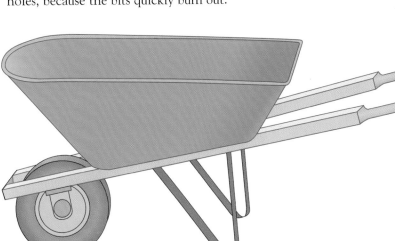

THE HARD FACTS ABOUT CONCRETE

Concrete is a mixture of sand, gravel, and portland cement that, when combined with water, sets into a unified, stonelike mass (*right*). Portland cement—a blend of pulverized, burned, then reground limestone, clay, and gypsum—is the glue that holds everything together. Water is the catalyst. Mixed with portland cement, it creates a chemical reaction called hydration, which causes the cement to harden, binding the sand and gravel.

Aggregates—the sand and gravel—make up about 70 percent of a concrete mix. A good mix should have enough fine sand to fill the spaces around the larger gravel. The various sizes of aggregate settle into a dense matrix held together by cement.

Concrete mixes are sized by the largest aggregate in the mix. Most projects call for concrete with medium-sized, ¾-inch aggregate. But as a rule, the largest aggregates should be no more than one-third the thickness of the concrete slab.

Aggregates should be free of dirt, which prevents the cement from bonding to them and weakens the mix. The water you mix with the concrete should be clean enough to drink.

WHAT TO ORDER: When ordering ready-mix concrete, ask the supplier to blend it to the following specifications:

■ **CEMENT:** The more portland cement in the mix, the stronger the concrete. Six sacks of cement per cubic yard of concrete is strong enough for most projects.

■ **WATER:** A water-to-cement ratio of 0.5 to 1 or 0.55 to 1 is best.

■ **SLUMP:** This term describes concrete consistency. It refers to the number of inches that a 12-inch-tall cone of fresh

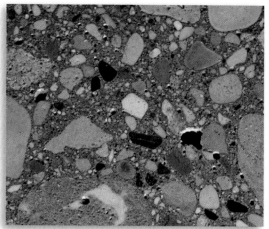

In this cross section of concrete, you can see how small aggregates, such as sand, fill in the spaces between larger aggregates to create a dense mass.

concrete spreads out or sags of its own weight. A 1-inch slump, from 12 to 11 inches, indicates a very stiff concrete mix. Concrete with a 10-inch slump is too soupy. Concrete with a 4-inch slump is good for most projects.

■ **STRENGTH:** Residential jobs require a load strength from 2,000 pounds per square inch (psi) to more than 4,000 psi. A six-sack mix with a water-to-cement ratio of 0.5 to 1 is plenty strong if it cures properly (*see page 39*).

ADDITIVES

Engineers and chemists have developed ways to modify concrete for specific purposes. For example, altering the ratio of ingredients creates concrete of different strengths. Using additives accelerates or retards setup time, prevents deterioration of a surface due to freezing and thawing, or makes the concrete mix workable in extreme heat or cold.

RIGHT ADDITIVE FOR THE JOB: Before mixing or ordering concrete, ask your supplier for advice on additives. Controlling the basic ingredients is the key to successful concrete work, but additives may help to adjust the concrete to certain conditions.

■ **AIR ENTRAINMENT:** This additive helps preserve concrete from freeze-thaw cycles in cold weather. Air-entrained concrete contains microscopic air cells, which help relieve internal pressures and prevent cracking. You can order air-entrained ready-mix, or you can add an air-entraining agent when mixing concrete in a mechanical mixer. But you can't mix it in by hand. Use only magnesium floats or darbies on air-entrained concrete—wood tears its surface.

A sturdy wheelbarrow is handy for mixing small amounts of concrete. Pour in the dry mix, then slowly add water as you stir with a shovel or hoe. The final product should have the same specifications as ready-mix concrete.

CALCULATING CONCRETE VOLUME

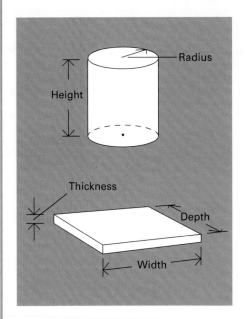

Radius

Height

Thickness

Depth

Width

Ready-mix concrete is sold by the "yard," meaning cubic yard—a cube that's 3 feet on all sides. After excavating, building forms, and pouring in gravel, take precise measurements of the project area, then calculate volume.

For rectangles, multiply length by width by depth (always all three dimensions), using feet and fractions of a foot rather than inches. Then divide by 27 to get the number of cubic yards (3 × 3 × 3 = 27). For example, if a patio slab will be 10 feet long, 8 feet wide, and 4 inches thick, multiply 10 × 8 × ⅓ to get 26.7 cubic feet, or about 1 (cubic) yard.

For cylindrical shapes, figure the area of the circle by multiplying π (3.14) by the radius squared. Multiply the result by the height of the cylinder. Again, measure in feet and fractions of a foot, and divide by 27 to find cubic yards.

To find the volume of complex shapes, mentally divide them into simpler shapes. Separately figure the volume of each shape, then add the totals. Add 10 percent to your total to account for irregularities.

It's better to have too much concrete mix than too little. Be prepared in case some concrete mix is left over. For example, have some forms for stepping-stones on hand to handle the excess.

■ **ACCELERATOR:** The accelerator of choice is calcium chloride. Accelerators make concrete set up faster on a cold day. They also reduce the risk of concrete freezing and cracking in cold weather.

■ **RETARDANT:** When the weather is hot and dry, use a retardant to slow the setting-up time for concrete.

■ **FIBERGLASS REINFORCEMENT:** Reinforcing additives may be available in your area, and for some projects, can take the place of steel reinforcement. Check with your local building department to see whether it is approved for your situation.

■ **WATER REDUCERS:** Sometimes called plasticizers, water reducers make concrete mix more workable and allow you to use 10 to 30 percent less water. Easy-to-work concrete results in less labor time on large jobs, and concrete made with less water is stronger.

REINFORCING STEEL

Concrete has great compressive strength—the ability to withstand crushing—but little tensile strength—the ability to withstand stretching or bending. This means that unreinforced concrete can crack easily. The solution is to embed steel reinforcing bars—rebar—or wire mesh in the concrete.

Rebar commonly comes in 20-foot lengths, in diameters of ⅜ inch (#3), ½ inch (#4), and ⅝ inch (#5), and in two grades of strength. Of these grades, 40 grade is adequate for most home projects; 60 grade is stronger.

You can bend rebar by hand. Have a helper stand on a board placed over the bar. Slip a pipe over one end of the bar to where you want the bend, then lift up on the pipe. There's also a tool designed to cut and bend rebar.

Rebar must be laid in the forms so that when encased in concrete, it is at least 3 inches away from soil and, aboveground, at least 1½ inches away from air. This spacing prevents the rebar from rusting and disintegrating over time.

Don't use bricks to hold rebar in place; they soak up and transfer moisture. Instead, place the rebar on concrete pavers or small blocks called "dobies," which have wires to hold on to the rebar.

When splicing rebar end-to-end, the pieces should overlap by 40 diameters' worth (20 inches for ½-inch rebar). Tie the bars together with wire wherever they intersect.

Don't pound vertical pieces of rebar into the ground. Instead, bend the ends into an L, then tie them to a horizontal bar or set them on dobies to keep the L at least 3 inches off the ground.

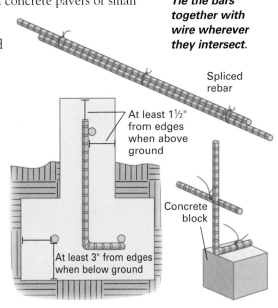

Spliced rebar

At least 1½" from edges when above ground

At least 3" from edges when below ground

Concrete block

THE HARD FACTS ABOUT CONCRETE

continued

For flat slabs, use concrete-reinforcing mesh made of #10 wire in a 6×6-inch grid (known as 6×6-inch 10/10 wire). It comes in rolls that are 5, 6, or 7 feet wide. Cut the mesh with wire cutters and work with it carefully. It can coil up viciously unless both ends are secure.

The building department has specifications for reinforcing steel—how much, which size, and exactly where to place it.

MIX YOUR OWN OR ORDER IT?

The excavation, forms, and rebar should be in place and inspected before you even think about ordering the concrete. Your options are buying the bulk ingredients and mixing the concrete yourself, buying premix concrete in bags, and ordering ready-mix for delivery.

Premix bags are convenient for very small jobs. The bags contain everything but the water. A 60-pound sack makes about ½ cubic foot (1/52 cubic yard). For patching and jobs where the concrete will be less than an inch thick, purchase sand-mix concrete.

As a rule, buying in bulk and mixing concrete yourself is cost-effective for amounts up to ¼ yard. Order ready-mix for any amount over 1 yard. For those awkward installations needing between ¼ and 1 yard, weigh the higher cost of ready-mixed delivery

Concrete isn't concrete until the sand, gravel, and cement are combined with water. You can do this yourself, using a wheelbarrow or mixer, but it's hard work. Other options include buying bags of the premixed dry ingredients or having ready-mix concrete delivered.

ANOTHER TYPE OF TRUCK

Standard concrete trucks with revolving barrels carry concrete that has already been mixed with water, so it's not practical to buy less than a yard at a time. A new type of truck carries the dry ingredients and makes the concrete mix on site. If available in your area, this may be the best solution for jobs requiring 1 yard or less of concrete.

against the inconvenience and effort of mixing. (One yard of concrete mix typically requires 564 pounds of cement, 1,400 pounds of sand, and 2,000 pounds of gravel.)

If you can, mix the job in sections. Combine the ingredients in a wheelbarrow or in a large plastic trough (or mortar box). For a large job, rent a machine mixer. Use the following recipe to make 1 cubic foot of standard mix: 2 shovelfuls of portland cement, 3–4 shovelfuls of sand, and 4–5 shovelfuls of aggregate. Typically, the cement will require 6 gallons of water per sack of cement. Add the water slowly; too much water will weaken the concrete.

To test your mix, place a shovelful of concrete on a piece of plywood. Slice through it with a trowel. If mixed properly, the mix should hold its shape yet remain soft enough to pour and form.

Bags of portland cement

Gravel

Sand

Supply of clean water

POST FOOTINGS

When building a deck, shed, or other structure, you'll direct most of your efforts to the carpentry work, but don't give short shrift to supporting the posts. Simply setting posts in a hole or on small precast piers (supports) could spell trouble. The structure could sink in one or more spots if the foundation on which the posts sit is not solid. And if you live where winters are cold, frost heave can raise the ground an inch or two every winter, cracking boards and damaging the structure.

Your local building department can advise you on the best method for installing post footings. The simplest way is to dig a posthole deeper than the frost line, set the post in it, and pour the concrete mix in. A better option is to set the posts above grade. Above grade, the post doesn't come in contact with the ground or standing water, so it lasts longer and is easier to replace, if necessary. You can also use shorter posts.

Dig the hole (deeper than the frost line), then insert a concrete tube form. Hold the form 2 to 4 inches above ground by nailing it to 2×4s lying on both sides of the hole. Fill the form with concrete mix, and while the mix is still wet, push a J-bolt into it, leaving about an inch of thread poking out.

After two or three days, when the concrete has set up, install a post anchor. Because it is difficult to dig holes and pour footings in exactly the right spot, choose an adjustable anchor so you can move it a couple of inches in either direction.

If you live in a warm area, you may be able to skip pouring a footing altogether. Instead, set the posts in the holes, fill with gravel or soil, and tamp very firmly.

LALLY POST

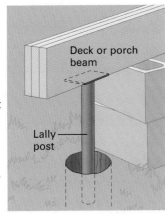

Here's an option that lets you set posts in concrete *after* the beams are in position. Typically used to shoulder sagging floor joists, Lallies are steel posts with support plates on top. First set your deck beams on temporary supports and position them precisely. Attach each Lally so it hangs from the beam into its post hole. Only after the posts are positioned perfectly do you cast them in concrete.

Deck or porch beam

Lally post

To support an air conditioner, spa, or other heavy equipment, a footed pad may be best. Excavate the area for the pad. Dig postholes within the pad area, then build a simple form for the pad from 2×4s. You may need to line the form with reinforcement mesh. Now you can pour the footings and pad at once.

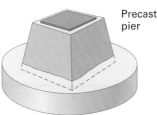

Precast pier

Instead of placing a precast pier on the ground, set it on a concrete footing.

Footings within the base keep a small pad foundation stable.

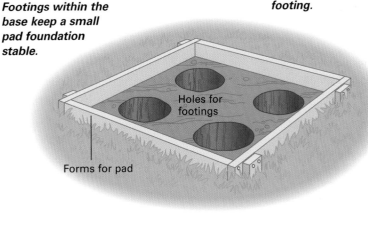

Holes for footings

Forms for pad

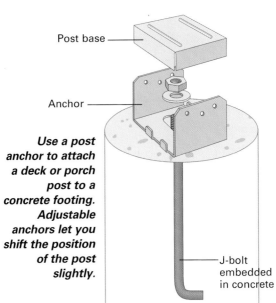

Post base

Anchor

Use a post anchor to attach a deck or porch post to a concrete footing. Adjustable anchors let you shift the position of the post slightly.

J-bolt embedded in concrete

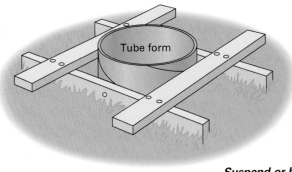

Tube form

Suspend or brace tube forms with 2×4s around the footing hole.

WALL FOOTINGS

Except for dry stone walls, every wall needs a footing to carry the structure's load. The footing is simply a concrete base that spreads the wall's weight over a broader footprint. These wall footings must extend below the local frost depth to prevent the wall from cracking when freezing and thawing make the ground shift.

For structures on slab foundations, such as garages and sheds, the slab's perimeter should be deeper than the rest of the slab to double as the footing. Perimeter footings, however, don't always need to extend below the frost line. Garages and sheds "float," rising and falling slightly during the changing seasons.

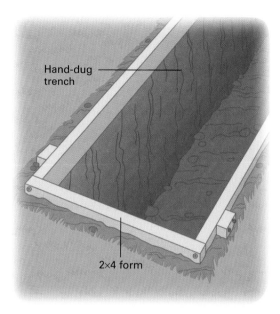

Dig footings for walls twice as wide as the wall and several inches longer. Build a form around the top of the footing for walls that stand entirely above ground.

The footing for an addition should be at the same depth as the house footing. To build a footing without first building forms, drive a stake next to the house to the height of the existing footing. Continue setting stakes in the footing, using a line level to keep them even with the first stake. Pour concrete just to the tops of the stakes for a level footing.

PLANNING FOOTINGS

Wall footings should be twice as wide as the wall and several inches longer on each end. Footings for most walls should be at least 12 inches deep, always below the frost line.

They must rest on soil that has not been excavated and is therefore firmly settled. Some building departments may require you to dig until you reach clay. Check local codes. If your soil is especially soft, you may need to build a larger-than-average footing.

Footings for walls—especially for retaining walls—need to incorporate a drainage system to keep water pressure from building up and damaging the wall. You'll find ways to provide drainage for footings on page 63.

To lay out the wall, follow the instructions on pages 16–17. For a deep footing, consider hiring someone to dig it. Hiring a pro may save you money: With a precise, professional hole, you'll need less concrete—and less liniment. Or for some heavy-duty fun, rent a backhoe or trench digger. (Check first for underground utilities and overhead wires.)

If your project will be inspected, dig the hole, lay any required reinforcing metal, and have an inspector approve it before you pour the concrete mix.

FORMING AND EXCAVATING

Forms hold concrete in a specific shape until it sets. For some projects, the form is the ground itself: a hole or trench dug to precise dimensions. Most forms are built from lumber or plywood (*see page 32*).

If a wall will be partly below grade— for example, a basement addition—you may get by without forms. Simply dig carefully.

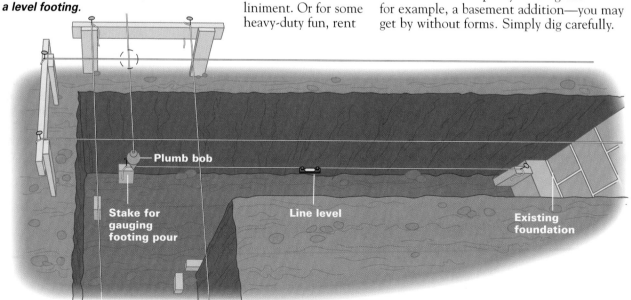

Plumb bob

Stake for gauging footing pour

Line level

Existing foundation

Set 2×4 forms before digging the footing. Use enough support stakes so the heavy concrete mix won't put a creative bow where you planned on straight edges.

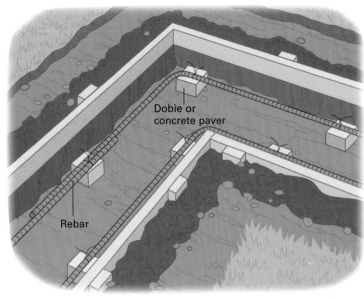

Dobie or concrete paver

Rebar

Concrete footings gain strength from reinforcing steel rods, or rebar. Position the rebar on concrete pavers or dobies so that it is encased in the poured footing.

However, for walls that are entirely above ground, forms allow you to bring the footing an inch or so above grade. For such forms use 2×4s nailed together to make a frame.

Set the form before you dig. Follow the layout lines to ensure that the sides are parallel. Also, place a level across the form every few feet to ensure that the sides are at the same height. Occasionally check for level along the length of each 2×4 as well.

Brace the form by driving 10-inch support stakes every 3 to 4 feet along the outside of the form; keep their tops below the upper edge of the form. Fasten the stakes to the form with screws or duplex nails.

Start digging. Take care to dig no deeper than necessary. A piece of tape on your spade makes a good depth guide. If you overdig and have to return some of the soil to the trench, be sure to tamp the surface thoroughly.

Footings must be level. On a sloped site, step down the footing so that each footing section is of a uniform depth. It often helps to use 2×8s for forms in a step-down situation. For strength, overlap the upper and lower forms by 2 feet or so. Excavate so that the footing is at the required depth at all points.

REINFORCEMENTS

A footing supports a lot of weight. Strengthen it with steel reinforcing rods, called rebar. It's common to use two parallel pieces of rebar. However, check local building codes; requirements vary.

Overlap the ends of the rebar by a foot or so, and wire them together in at least two places (*see page 23*). Use dobies or concrete pavers to hold the rebar off the ground at least 3 inches.

For a sloped site, footings must step down. Use 2×8 lumber, overlapping upper and lower forms by 2 feet.

For an unformed footing (above), create the step-down with a plywood barrier firmly staked to the sides of the trench.

PERIMETER FOUNDATIONS

A simple foundation for a garage, shed, or basement addition is within the capabilities of most do-it-yourselfers. You can build a slab foundation, which must be on level ground, or a perimeter foundation, which will work on irregular ground. A perimeter foundation resembles an inverted T, with a wide, continuous footing as its base and a narrow "stem" wall rising above the base. This construction allows you to pour the footing and the wall at the same time—a "monolithic pour."

For a single-story structure, most codes require that the footing be 12 inches wide and the stem wall 6 inches wide. The footing for a two-story building should be 15 inches wide, the wall 8 inches wide. Footings should be as thick as the wall is wide and 12 inches below grade or below the frost line. The stem wall should rise at least 8 inches above grade. If you need a stem wall higher than 3 feet, call in a pro.

Use batter boards and mason's line to align forms for a perimeter foundation. Steel foundation stakes are easy to drive plumb and to remove.

LAYOUT AND EXCAVATION

Using the techniques described on pages 16–17, mark the outside edges of the stem wall with mason's line. Build the batter boards tall enough that string lines for the walls clear the top of the forms. Level all lines.

Steel foundation stake

3" gap

Once the trench is dug and the metal stakes are placed, attach form boards, starting with the exterior walls. The bottoms of the form boards should line up with the top of the footing.

Cleat

Brace

Anchor bolt

Form tie with wedge

USING RENTED FORMS

Renting concrete forms can save time and make it easier to keep the walls straight. A concrete company may rent them out, or look under "concrete forms" in the yellow pages. Forms are available in a variety of sizes. You may need to combine sizes. These forms go together with steel form ties and wedges. Oil the forms so they're easy to remove from the hardened concrete.

Using a plumb bob and tape measure, mark the location of the trench with flour or sand. The marks should be 3 inches outside the wall's string line for a 12-inch-wide footing, 3½ inches for a 15-inch-wide footing.

Remove the line and dig the footing. Its sides should be straight, its bottom level, and the corners square. Use 2×4 form boards if necessary. If the ground slopes, prepare step-down footings (*see page 27*). Reattach the lines to check your work—the stem wall must be centered over the footing. Finally, install rebar reinforcement.

FORMS FOR THE STEM WALL

Start with the exterior forms. Remove the interior string line. Drive 3- to 4-foot-long stakes—steel foundation stakes with holes for nails, or 1×2s—at 3- to 4-foot intervals along the footing trench. Steel stakes are easier to drive into soil and easier to pull out of fresh concrete. Place the interior face of each stake 1½ inches outside the string line for the wall, to allow room for the 2-by form boards.

LEVELING: With a helper, hold the top form board in position. Secure the board to the stakes with two 8-penny (8d) duplex nails or 2-inch screws. Check frequently to ensure that the top of the form is even with the mason's line. Then add the lower courses, checking for level as you go and leaving space between each course for form ties. Boards on the ends can extend beyond the corner; you'll butt the boards of intersecting walls against them. The lowest board should extend slightly into the trench.

BRACES: Every 4 feet and at every corner, support the form with an angle brace made from 2×4s. Attach one end of each brace to the top of the form. Align the forms with the mason's line, then drive a short stake into the ground at the bottom end of the brace to hold the form in place. Nail the stake to the brace.

INTERIOR FORMS: To make interior form walls, string new lines between the batter boards, this time 6 inches inside the exterior form (or 8 inches for 15-inch-wide footings). Drive foundation stakes 1½ inches outside that line, then begin hanging the forms the same way you hung the exterior wall forms.

TIES: After all the boards for the interior wall are in place, connect the two walls every 3 to 4 feet along the top with 1×4 cleats. Because cleats double as anchor holders, locate one wherever an anchor is needed.

Connect the lower courses with steel form ties. These ties are comprised of a strap and a wedge. They hold the walls exactly 6 (or 8) inches apart. The strap fits into the cracks between boards, and the wedges fit into the straps on the outside of the form to lock the straps into place. Space the form ties under the top course 3 feet apart. They should be 2 feet apart for the lower courses.

FORMING OPENINGS

To access the crawl space under the structure you're building, leave an opening in the wall. Construct a three-sided box—the form for the opening—of pressure-treated lumber. Use 2×6s for a 6-inch-thick wall. For an opening at the bottom of the wall, place the box within the form so that its "legs" point down with their tips just below ground level. Drive a few nails through the form and into the box to hold it in place during the pour.

If you plan to run water, electricity, or heating ducts underground into the new structure, create holes in the footing. Lay a length of electrical conduit or plastic drainpipe across the footing trench, extending it about 12 inches beyond the footing on each side. Wrap the pipe with blanket insulation or roofing felt before the pour to cushion it from the expansion and contraction of the hardening concrete.

Have the local building department inspect everything before you order and pour the concrete mix. Clear all debris from the trenches, and coat the inside of the forms with form oil, using a pump sprayer or a paintbrush. Oiling the forms makes them easier to remove. Make sure that the rebar is encased in concrete so it is separated from soil by 3 inches and air by 1½ inches. Drill ⅝-inch holes in the cleats, and hang J-bolt anchors from them. Order concrete that is stiff—tell the company that you are making a monolithic pour—a stiff mix doesn't well up out of the footing.

POURING AND FINISHING

For the pour, have a minimum of two but preferably four helpers on hand. (*To learn about pouring techniques, see pages 34–35.*) Fill the forms, consolidate the concrete mix (remove air pockets by plunging rebar up and down in the mix and tapping the sides of the form), then screed and float the top. When the concrete is hard enough to hold its shape, pull the stakes. The hardened concrete keeps the forms from collapsing. Leave the forms in place for 48 to 72 hours.

Pour perimeter foundations in two passes, one to fill the footing and the other to fill the wall.

Remove air bubbles in the footing by plunging rebar in the cement mix.

Once the wall is poured, do plenty of poking and banging to eliminate air pockets.

Stem wall

Footing

SLAB FOUNDATIONS

Concrete slabs are the basis for many structures. They function as floor and foundation for garages and sheds. Concrete patios, driveways, and sidewalks are little more than slabs. And slabs can be the substrate for tile or mortared stone.

A slab is simpler to make than a perimeter foundation. It must be located on ground that is level or nearly so, and all rough electrical and plumbing work must be completed before pouring the concrete. The next 10 pages take you through the steps for building a slab, the first of which is to have the location of buried utility lines marked on your property. Read this entire section before tackling any major concrete project.

Anatomy of a slab foundation: The solid slab rests on undisturbed soil and a firm gravel and sand base. Rebar in the footing and mesh in the slab add strength. To support walls, a perimeter footing is needed. J-bolts allow for attaching a 2×4 wall plate. Plastic sheeting retards the curing process, strengthening the concrete.

SAVE YOUR BACK

Concrete work offers plenty of opportunities for damaging your back. If you are not accustomed to such abuse, a day of digging with a spade, pushing wheelbarrows, or even screeding and floating can cause you to wake up the next morning in agony. Take it easy: Take breaks and get lots of help.

PLANNING

How thick to make the slab, as well as the amount and type of reinforcement to use, depends on the slab's function. For sidewalks and patios, a 3-inch slab with no reinforcement is fine—although 3½ inches reinforced with 6-inch mesh is preferable. Driveway and garage slabs should be at least 4 inches thick with reinforcing mesh. Where the driveway meets the street, the slab should be 6 inches or thicker. Make slabs supporting walls at least 12 inches thick with rebar reinforcement and a 4- to 8-inch bed of compacted gravel. Local code may require a sand bed as well.

Plan for drainage. If you don't want water to puddle on the slab, construct it so that it slopes 1 inch for every 10 feet. To avoid water accumulating around the base of the slab, provide an outlet for the runoff. A mulched flower or shrub border at the perimeter may do the trick. To handle large amounts of runoff, however, dig a trench around the slab and fill it with gravel. For seriously wet sites, also embed a perforated drainpipe in the trench (*see page 47*). Freestanding slabs, such as sidewalks, should have a crown (be slightly higher in the center) so water flows to both sides.

LAYING OUT AND DIGGING

Follow the directions on pages 16 and 17 to set batter boards and mason's lines to mark the perimeter of the slab, checking for square and adjusting for slope. (A charged—water-filled—garden hose works well for laying out curved lines.) Use the crosspieces on the batter boards to adjust for slope, lowering them as necessary. Then trace the perimeter onto the ground by sprinkling sand, lime, or flour under the mason's line.

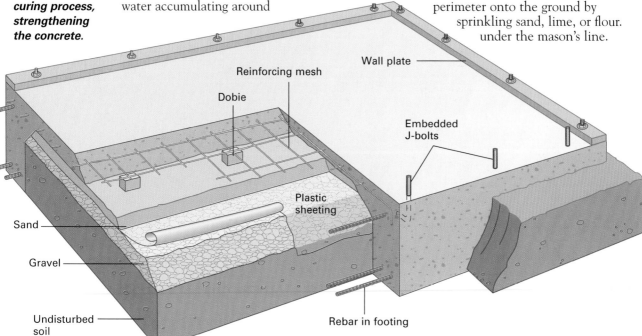

Reinforcing mesh

Dobie

Wall plate

Embedded J-bolts

Plastic sheeting

Sand

Gravel

Undisturbed soil

Rebar in footing

If the slab abuts the house, snap a chalk line to indicate the slab's height on the house foundation. It should be about an inch below the door threshold so snow and rain won't enter your home. Include the thickness of any tiles or stones that go on top of the slab.

Next, take down the strings. Remove the sod around the perimeter, then dig a trench 3 inches beyond the outside edge of the slab to allow room for the forms.

At this point, you can construct the forms (*see pages 32–33*), taking care to keep them level or properly sloped, or continue on with batter boards.

If you build the forms, you can then use them to attach lines from which to measure the excavation. Otherwise, install more batter boards, ringing the slab with them, and reattach lines to them. String a grid of 4- to 5-foot squares across the slab (*see below*). The grid makes it easy to take height measurements as you excavate, install the gravel base, and build forms.

Excavate the area to a uniform depth that allows for a 4- to 8-inch gravel base and the thickness of the slab. (In most cases, the slab will be an inch or two above grade.) You may need to dig a footing around the perimeter as well, depending on how you will use the slab and depending on local building codes.

Use a spade for small excavations; rent a backhoe or dump loader for larger projects. Take frequent measurements to avoid overdigging. Finish with a square spade, getting the bottom smooth and the edges square (the cleaner the excavation, the less wasted concrete). Moisten the entire area, and tamp it with a vibrating tamper or a hand tamper.

Roughly lay out the perimeter footing. Dribble sand or flour over a charged garden hose to mark a curve.

Snap a chalk line on the house foundation to mark the topmost level of the slab.

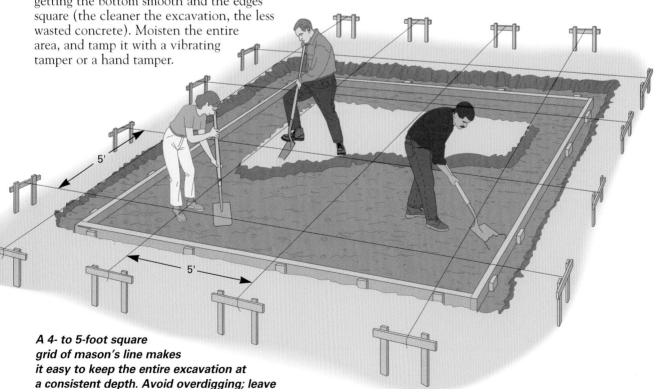

A 4- to 5-foot square grid of mason's line makes it easy to keep the entire excavation at a consistent depth. Avoid overdigging; leave the floor of the excavation as undisturbed as possible.

SLAB FOUNDATIONS
continued

LAYING A GRAVEL BASE

For a slab to remain stable, the concrete mix must be poured on a solid bed of gravel, especially in areas with severe winter frost heaves. You can add the gravel after building the forms, but often it is easier to install the gravel base after excavating the slab and before the forms are in the way.

Spread a 4-inch layer of crushed rock or class-5 pea gravel on top of the firm soil base. Rake it evenly, then wet it down and pack it with a vibrating power tamper or a plate compactor. A hand tamper is adequate for a small job. Do a thorough job, going over every spot at least twice. Repeat this process until the gravel is at the correct depth—4 inches below the finished surface—and feels solid.

BUILDING FORMS

Concrete is a versatile but unforgiving substance. It fills excavations and forms exactly. It also reproduces mistakes exactly. If you install forms that tilt, warp, or bulge, you'll regret it. So take the time to build them correctly.

Construct the forms out of straight 2×4 lumber. For permanent forms, use treated or rot-resistant wood. If possible, buy lumber that is long enough to span the entire excavation so you won't have to butt joints.

The 2×4s are actually 3½ inches—not 4 inches—wide, so for a 4-inch-thick slab you'll need to backfill some gravel or tack

Concrete is heavy. It has an outward thrust of 150 psi, so stake or brace forms carefully. Drive stakes at least every 4 feet, closer together on curves. At joints, nail all forms to one stake, or stake and brace as shown here. Permanent dividers serve as control joints.

scraps of lumber along the bottom of the forms to prevent concrete from seeping under them. Even though below grade, this concrete will make it hard for grass or other plants to grow. When pouring a thicker slab, use 2×6s or larger boards for the forms.

Align the inside edges of the forms directly under the perimeter string lines. Drive stakes—2×2, 2×4, or steel—into the ground every 3 feet on the outside of the forms, and attach them to the form boards with 16d duplex nails or 2½-inch deck screws. The stakes must be strong because they'll likely be bumped during construction. Wherever two forms meet end-to-end, drive a support stake at the joint and fasten both form boards to it.

To ensure that the forms slope properly to allow water run off, follow the layout lines. You can also use a carpenter's level and a long straightedge to determine slope. Forms should slope 1 inch for every 10 feet.

There are two ways to make curved forms. For a tight curve, where you're simply rounding off a corner, build the forms as you would for a rectangle. Cut a strip of sheet metal or thin hardboard. Bend it around the corner and nail it to the form boards. Stake the strip for support. For larger curves, use two to three layers of 4-inch-wide strips of ¼-inch hardboard or plywood. The extra layers will provide strength. Cut them longer than they need to be, position them to follow the curve, and then stake them to hold them in place.

Use an expansion strip against the house foundation. This keeps the new concrete from bonding with the house concrete and cracking it as the slab expands.

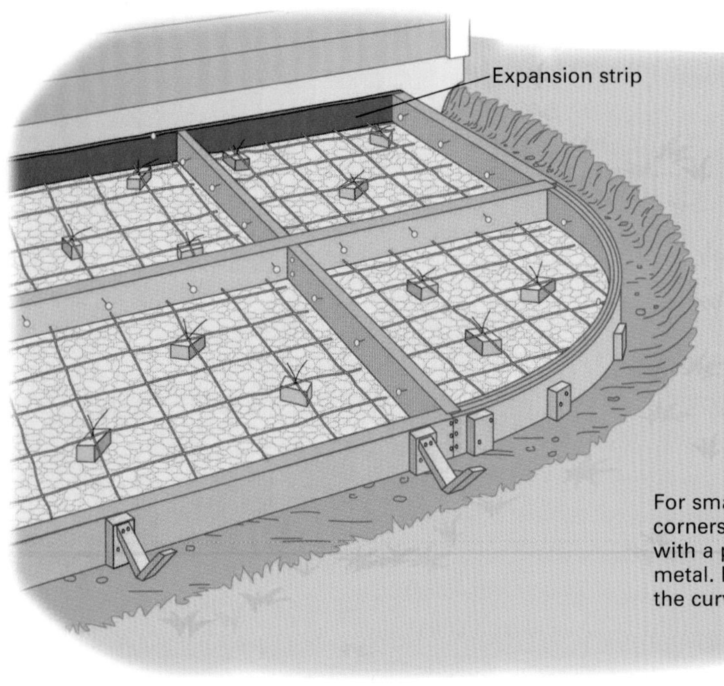

Expansion strip

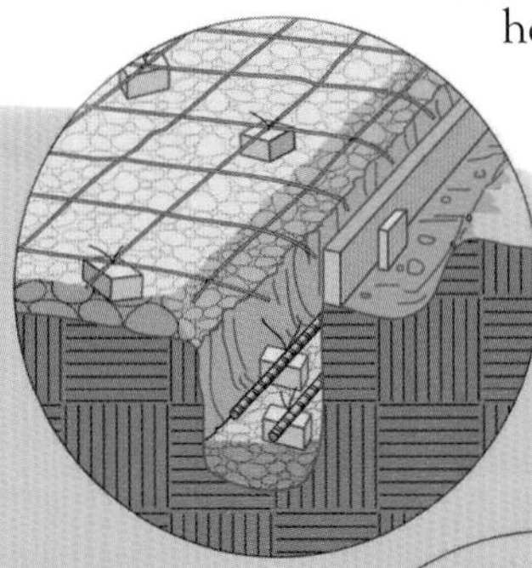

If your area is subject to ground heave, dig a perimeter footing. In cold climates, extend it beneath the frost line.

For small, rounded corners, form the curve with a piece of sheet metal. Backfill soil behind the curve for support.

SUPPORTING A LIGHTWEIGHT STRUCTURE

If your slab will support a lightweight structure, such as a sunshade, arbor, or trellis, it requires posts with concrete footings. When laying out the patio forms, mark each post location, and deepen the excavation an additional 6 to 12 inches at those points. Do not fill the holes with gravel. After you pour the concrete and it begins to set up, embed a post anchor or column base in the concrete, making sure that it is properly aligned. (See page 25 for more about post footings.)

If the slab will support a garage or other heavy structure, the requirements are more stringent. Instead of simply using anchors, you must provide a reinforced perimeter foundation for the slab and install a sill plate to anchor the walls.

Although not required for patios, it doesn't hurt to reinforce the slab with 6-inch mesh. The mesh will help prevent the concrete from cracking with changes in the weather. Lay the mesh on 2-inch dobies so that it is centered in the concrete. If you've built a perimeter foundation around the slab, reinforce the footing with $\frac{3}{8}$- or $\frac{1}{2}$-inch rebar, setting it on 3-inch dobies. Check with your local building department for specific requirements for both mesh and rebar.

PERMANENT FORMS

For some slabs, especially for patios, the forms are permanent, serving as a decorative edging. Many patios also have wood strips dividing the concrete. These function as expansion or control joints, and they provide a guide for screeding large areas of concrete. If you mix your own concrete, they can make your job easier, allowing you to work in stages, pouring only part of the slab at a time. Permanent dividers should be no more than 10 feet apart.

Make permanent forms and divider strips with pressure-treated lumber rated "ground contact" or "CCA 0.40" or greater. You can also use redwood, but it is expensive.

Join the boards at the corners with neat butt joints (miter joints come apart over time). Drive any interior stakes at least 1 inch below the tops of the forms so they'll be covered with concrete. Secure them to the forms with 16d hot-dipped galvanized (HDG) nails. Also drive 16d HDG nails or deck screws horizontally into the boards at midheight every 16 inches where concrete will be poured against them. These anchor the boards to the concrete. Cover the top edges of the forms with masking tape to prevent the concrete from staining the wood.

If your slab will be wider than 10 feet and you won't be using permanent wood dividers, stake a 2×4 in place to use as a temporary screed guide. Place the guide at the same height as the forms so that you will be able to drag a screed board across it. Once you have run the screed over the surface, remove the guide.

— Duplex nail

Below left: For slabs wider than 10 feet, install a temporary screed guide.

Below right: Don't rely on stakes alone to support a slab form. Instead, brace the stakes with 1×4s.

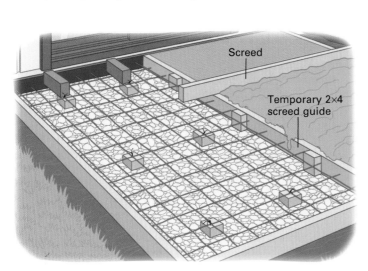

Screed

Temporary 2×4 screed guide

SLAB FOUNDATIONS
continued

Right: On a typical pour, one person (perhaps the truck driver) fills the wheelbarrows.

A slab of any size is a serious undertaking. You'll be dealing with a large amount of cement mix, and you'll have to place, consolidate, and finish it in quick order. Here are the keys to success.

POURING CONCRETE

Take special care to prepare your site before the ready-mix truck arrives. If possible, have the truck back in and pour directly into the forms. Be aware, however, that concrete trucks are very heavy and can seriously damage lawns and driveways. If you'll be hauling the mix by wheelbarrow, make sturdy paths from 2×10 or 2×12 planks or strips of plywood.

Pouring a slab calls for teamwork. While one person hauls the concrete mix, another shovels it into place, and a third consolidates it. Start screeding as soon as the concrete is poured. With a smaller team, finish one section before pouring the next.

Before the truck arrives, decide who will handle the truck arm, who will handle wheelbarrows, who will spread concrete, who will consolidate it, and who will screed. The truck driver may or may not help direct the flow of concrete into forms or wheelbarrows; check with the company.

You will need to signal the driver to start and stop the flow of concrete. Because of the length of the chute, a fair amount of concrete will continue to run out of the chute after the flow has been stopped. So anticipate this overflow. Scrape the chute clean with a scrap of wood when you finish filling a wheelbarrow to prevent concrete from dribbling on the ground between fillings.

Concrete mix is amazingly heavy. It's not unusual for a first-timer to lose control of a loaded wheelbarrow and dump it on the lawn. Start with small loads—about half full—and increase the load as you feel more comfortable. The cardinal rule: As soon as you start losing control of the wheelbarrow, push down on its handles with both hands.

Before pouring, wet down the trenches, gravel bed, and forms so they won't absorb moisture from the concrete. Pour the forms farthest from the truck first, filling to the tops of the forms and using shovels to distribute the mix. Do not throw the mix. Place it carefully to keep aggregates from separating, which weakens the concrete.

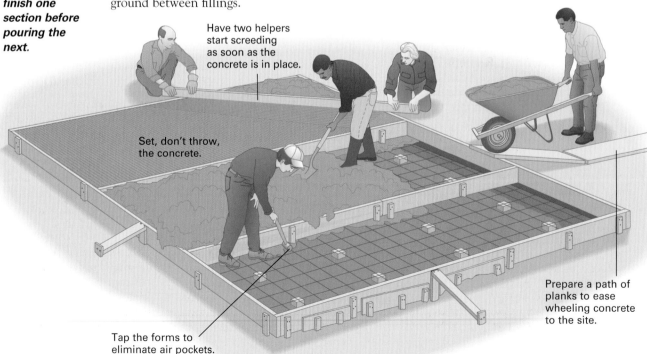

Have two helpers start screeding as soon as the concrete is in place.

Set, don't throw, the concrete.

Prepare a path of planks to ease wheeling concrete to the site.

Tap the forms to eliminate air pockets.

Consolidate—or settle—the concrete mix by jabbing a shovel or rod up and down in it. For maximum strength and durability, the mix must be dense but not packed. Make sure the wire mesh or rebar remains centered between the gravel base and the finished surface. You may have to occasionally pull it up with a shovel or garden rake.

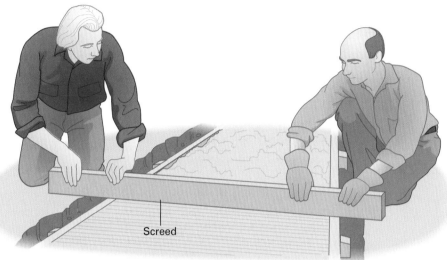

Screed

SCREEDING

After filling the forms, level the concrete so it is even with the top of the forms— a process known as screeding, or striking off. Place a straight 2×4 across the forms (or temporary screed guides, if using them). Draw the board forward with a side-to-side sawing motion. If there are humps in the surface after the first pass, screed again. If low spots remain, fill them with concrete mix, consolidate the mix, then screed the low spot. To finish, remove temporary guides; shovel concrete mix into the cavity they leave behind, then consolidate and screed the area.

Use a straight piece of 2×4 to screed the surface, pulling it forward with a firm side-to-side sawing motion.

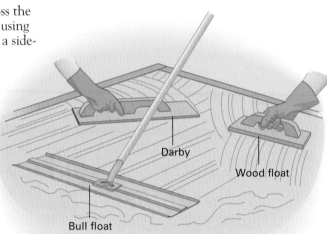

Darby

Bull float

Wood float

Start the smoothing process by floating the concrete with a darby, a wood float, or a bull float.

FLOATING

The next step, a preliminary smoothing called floating, pushes aggregates below the concrete surface. For small areas that you can reach easily as you kneel by the slab, use a regular hand float or an elongated darby, which extends your reach about 2 feet. For large slabs, use a bull float—a wide, flat float attached to a long handle. All three types are made from either magnesium or wood. Magnesium floats resist sticking better. Always use a magnesium float for air-entrained concrete.

To use a float, push it away from you with the leading edge slightly raised so it doesn't dig in. Pull it back in the same manner with the leading edge raised. Overlap each pass until you have gone over the entire slab.

Finish each section up to this point before starting the next section. Avoid pouring new concrete against concrete that has already set up. This creates a cold joint, which fractures easily and is unsightly as well.

Floating causes water to rise to the surface, but don't let this fool you into thinking that you have plenty of time to work. While one or more people continue to do the floating, the finisher should get to work as quickly as possible.

ARE YOU REALLY READY? A CHECKLIST

Readiness is the watchword when it comes to pouring concrete. Before the truck arrives, be entirely sure that you have all your ducks in a row. Here's a basic list of tools and materials you need. Your job may call for other items as well.

☐ **Tools:** Hose, buckets, wheelbarrows, shovels, screed boards, hammers, wood or magnesium floats, darby and bull float (if needed), magnesium trowels, steel trowels, edger, jointer.
☐ **Materials:** Anchor bolts or post anchors (if needed), planks to make paths for the wheelbarrows. All wire mesh and rebar should be in place before the pour.
☐ **Helpers:** At the very least, two. Unless you have experience, hire a concrete finisher. See that you and your helpers are clothed properly, with gloves and tight-fitting rubber boots for those who will wade into the wet concrete.

SLAB FOUNDATIONS
continued

EDGING AND JOINTING

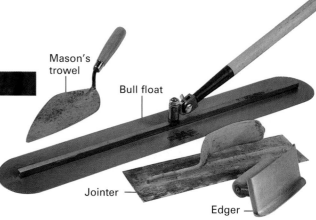

Mason's trowel

Bull float

Jointer

Edger

After floating the slab, separate the concrete from the form by slipping a mason's trowel between the two and drawing it along the form. Cut in deeply if you will ultimately remove the forms, but slice down only an inch or so around a permanent form.

Next, where you'll remove the forms, smooth and round the top edges of the concrete with an edging tool or edger. This not only improves the appearance of the slab, but it also helps to compact the concrete along the perimeter. Also, rounded edges don't readily crack or chip.

Hold the edger flat on the concrete surface with its curved edge pressed against the form. Work it in short back-and-forth strokes, always tilting the leading edge up slightly and applying medium pressure. After finishing an edge, go over it again using long, smooth strokes.

CONTROL JOINTS: Concrete exposed to weather swells and shrinks with the seasons, resulting in irregular cracks in the slab. Control joints provide a place for the slab to crack in a controlled way—along a straight line and under the joint so the crack isn't visible on the surface.

After edging the slab, cut control joints, or grooves, into the surface of the concrete. (You can skip this step if your slab is in an enclosed area, such as a garage, or if you have installed permanent wood dividers.)

Use a jointer, working it in the same way as you did the edger. Don't try to cut a control joint without a guide; the joint will turn out sloppy looking. To make a guide, lay a straight board across the forms. You can also wait until the concrete has hardened but not cured (half a day is usually about right). Using a straight 2×4 as a guide, cut a line with a circular saw equipped with a masonry blade.

Make control joints fairly deep—about one-fourth as deep as the thickness of the concrete. For patios, place control joints every 10 feet in both directions; for walks, at intervals equal to $1\frac{1}{2}$ times their width (every $4\frac{1}{2}$ feet for a 3-foot-wide walk).

APPLYING THE FINAL FINISH

Depending on weather conditions, you may have as little as an hour (in hot, dry weather) or as much as half a day (in cool, humid weather) to smooth the slab surface. Consider hiring a professional concrete finisher to help on large jobs. Smaller jobs offer a better opportunity to learn this skill yourself.

Important: Wait until the sheen of water on the surface of the concrete disappears before you attempt the final finish. Evaporation can take minutes in hot, dry weather or more than an hour when it's damp and cool. Finishing while water remains on the surface results in concrete that is dusty or that spalls or has other problems after it has cured.

If you notice that the concrete is beginning to set up before the sheen has disappeared, sweep off the water with a push broom, soak it up with burlap, or drag the surface of the concrete with a hose. Whichever method you use, don't step on the wet concrete.

Finishing is performed with various tools and techniques, depending on the texture you want for the slab. For a slightly rough texture, refloat the surface with a float. Steel troweling creates a slick surface, like that on basement

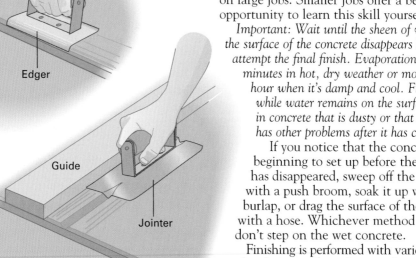

Separate the concrete from the form by cutting along their boundary with a mason's trowel.

Form

Edger

Use a guide to make a crossways joint. When using a jointer or edger, make one pass using short, back-and-forth strokes, then follow up with long strokes.

Guide

Jointer

floors. Although it's not the best finish for an outdoor slab, troweling is the first step when creating some types of rough finishes.

To achieve a smooth steel-trowel finish, hand-trowel the surface two or three times. The concrete should be hard enough to support your weight on knee boards but fresh enough to produce a moistened paste as you work. Keep track of the concrete's wetness. If it gets too dry, it becomes unworkable. Overworking it when it is very wet can cause the top layer to flake off later on.

Start troweling from the edge of the slab. Get into a comfortable position so you won't have to overreach. Do as much as you can from the lawn, then use a kneeling board to work in the middle.

Hold the steel trowel almost flat, with the leading edge raised slightly. Use long, sweeping arcs. Don't press hard. Overlap each succeeding arc by half the tool's length.

One finish that you begin by steel-troweling is brooming. It creates a patterned nonslip surface. Trowel the concrete, then drag a dampened broom across it in straight lines, curves, or waves. Soft brooms designed for this purpose produce a shallow pattern. Stiff-bristled brooms cut deeper. After grooming the surface, you may need to touch up the edges and control joints.

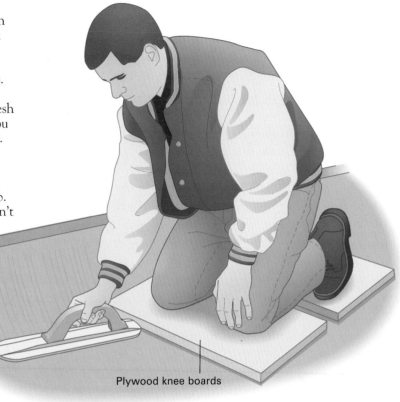

Plywood knee boards

Keep knees and toes from digging into the wet concrete by resting them on boards. Use two boards, or one board large enough to accommodate both knees and toes. Have a second set of boards handy so you can move around without stopping.

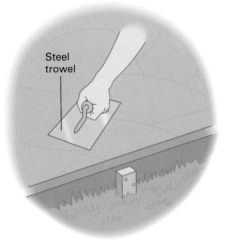

Steel trowel

For a an extra-smooth surface, finish with a steel trowel.

POWER FINISHER

In hot weather, the concrete may harden faster than you can finish it by hand. The solution: Rent a power finisher, also known as a helicopter or whirlybird. This equipment will allow you to produce a fairly smooth finish over large areas, even if you're not a skilled finisher. You'll still need to edge and joint the slab, and you might need to hand-finish small areas.

Pull broom toward you.

The coarser the broom bristles, the rougher the surface will be. Always pull the broom toward you; never push it away. Don't overlap broom strokes; that creates an irregular effect.

SLAB FOUNDATIONS
continued

CUSTOM FINISHES

Floating, troweling, and brooming are only three of the many ways to produce decorative concrete surfaces. Here are some others.

SEEDED-AGGREGATE FINISH: Divide the project into manageable segments so the concrete mix doesn't harden before you can work in the stones. Pour the concrete so its surface is about ½ inch below the top of the forms; then screed, float, and finish it.

Sprinkle aggregate evenly over the slab. With a helper, press the aggregate into the concrete with long 2×6s or flat shovels. Embed the stones firmly so their tops are just visible. If necessary, go over them with a wood float to push them down more.

When the concrete has hardened enough to support your weight on knee boards, re-move excess concrete around the stones with a stiff nylon brush or broom. Work carefully so you don't dislodge the stones. Remove the debris, spray a curing agent over the slab, then cover it with a plastic sheet.

After the concrete curs for 24 hours, repeat the brooming followed by a fine spray of water to expose about half of each stone. The spray should be strong enough to wash away the concrete loosened by the broom but not dislodge the stones. Let the aggregate dry for a couple of hours, then hose off any film that develops on the stones. Again, cover the area with plastic so it can cure slowly. After curing, remove any haze on the aggregate with muriatic acid.

HAND-TOOLED FINISH: Float the slab, then make geometric or random lines in the finished concrete with a joint-strike tool (*see above*). If you need to re-trowel part of the surface, be sure to strike the lines again.

STAMPED FINISH: Use a steel or rubber stamping tool to produce patterns resembling brick, cobblestone, flagstone, and others.

First, measure the base of the stamp and adjust spacing so the pattern comes out evenly. Increase efficiency by using two stamps side by side. Set both stamps in place. Stand on one, then step over to the other. The impressions should be about 1 inch deep. Smooth out the edges of the pattern with a joint-strike tool.

Joint-strike tool for hand-tooling

1. Spread aggregate.

2. Embed stones.

3. Smooth and settle stones with a wood float.

4. Sweep off excess concrete as the surface sets up.

5. Wash excess concrete from stones with a fine water spray.

When adding the stones for a seeded-aggregate finish, the concrete must be wet and workable. Divide the project into manageable sections so that the concrete doesn't harden before you can get to it. As you work, take care to not dislodge the stones by sweeping too vigorously or using too strong of a water spray.

Concrete stamp

Create the effect of a stone walk by pressing a concrete stamp into the mix. Many patterns are available.

CURING CONCRETE

Although concrete will harden in a day, it doesn't reach adequate strength until it has cured for at least five to seven days. During this time, it must be protected from drying out. Concrete that dries too quickly will not be strong.

COVER IT: To prevent evaporation, cover the concrete with plastic. If the temperature is cool, use black plastic because it absorbs heat from the sun. Weight the edges of the plastic and any seams with small stones or boards to trap as much moisture as possible. Let the concrete remain protected for at least five to seven days.

KEEP IT WET: If you are able to attend to your slab regularly, sprinkling it with water is better than covering it with plastic. Cover the slab with old blankets or burlap, and wet them down often enough that they stay wet. Or, water the concrete directly. To keep the water drops from pitting the surface, wait until the concrete is fairly hard before spraying it.

USE A CURING AGENT: To facilitate curing, spray or roll a curing agent onto the slab. Clear or tinted white, these agents keep the concrete moist. Don't use a curing agent if you plan to cover your slab with tile, bricks, stone, or flooring materials. Mortar and tile adhesive will not stick to the treated concrete.

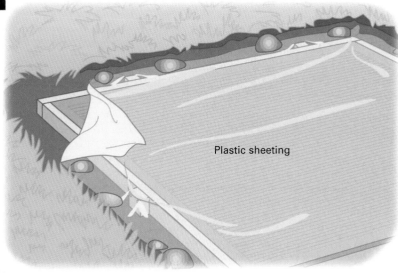

Plastic sheeting

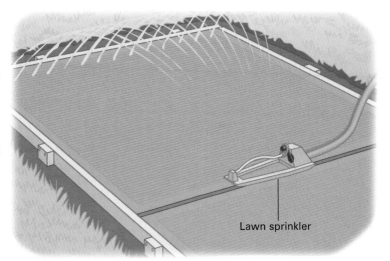

Lawn sprinkler

Cover fresh concrete with plastic to stop evaporation while the concrete cures.

Watering the slab with a sprinkler or a hose is effective, as long as you are able to keep close tabs on things. Neither soak the slab nor let it dry out.

COLORING CONCRETE

Many people color stamped concrete, as well as other types of concrete. To add color to concrete, use a coloring agent. These are pigments, which are available from most concrete suppliers. Mix the agent throughout the entire batch of concrete mix. Or pour uncolored concrete mix to within 1 inch of the top of the form, then mix pigment into the mix for the final layer.

You can also color freshly poured concrete before it hardens by sprinkling a powdered coloring agent over it, then hand-floating the dissolved powder into the surface. Repeat the process until the color reaches the shade you want.

Straw

If there is a possibility of freezing weather, cover curing concrete with straw or insulating blankets. For cool but not freezing conditions, use black plastic.

BACKYARD BASKETBALL COURT

Using the techniques from the previous pages, you can build a backyard basketball court one weekend and shoot hoops with the kids the next.

A regulation high school court is 84 feet long by 50 feet wide, but you don't need nearly that much space for a backyard court. The minimum size for two-on-two play is 20×20 feet; 15×20 feet will do for one-on-one or games of "horse." Whatever size court you build, the free-throw line must be 15 feet from the backboard. Try to orient the court so that the sun won't be in shooters' eyes in the afternoon, when you are most likely to play.

The hoop should be 10 feet above the concrete surface. You can buy a backboard mounted on a movable base, which allows you to move it out of the way if necessary. But be prepared for a sizable investment. Or you can permanently install an adjustable-height pole. Both types are available at sporting goods stores. To help avoid injuries, wrap the pole with foam padding.

GENERAL DIRECTIONS

The minimum size for a basketball court is 15 by 20 feet. Free-throw lanes should be 12 feet wide and 15 feet from the backboard.

Lay out the slab for the court, build forms, and excavate the slab. Then dig the hole for the pole. Locate it so the backboard over-hangs the court by about 15 to 20 inches and is centered on the end. Most poles require a hole about 3 feet deep by 18 inches in diameter, but manufacturers usually supply installation instructions. Add a few inches of gravel to the hole and tamp it.

Place the pole in the center of the hole, snugging the pole in place with stones. With a level, plumb up the pole, using the stones as wedges. A post level, which tests for plumb in two directions at once, is handy for this task. (Make sure the top of the pole is capped so that water doesn't get in.)

Once the pole is plumb and secure, pour the concrete. Mound it up an inch or so above grade and slope it away from the pole so that rainwater runs away from the pole. Cut control joints, then finish the slab. A smooth, steel-troweled finish is the best surface for a court. Complete directions for working with concrete are on pages 30–39.

Let the concrete cure for five days, then install the backboard and hoop on the pole. Draw lines for the free-throw lane by snapping chalk lines using the dimensions in the illustration. For 1-inch-wide lines, strike two lines 1 inch apart. Mask the outside edge of both lines, then carefully apply a coat of masonry paint between the taped lines.

Install a pole in a hole roughly 3 feet deep and 18 inches in diameter. Pour the concrete about 1 inch above grade, sloping it away from the pole with a trowel.

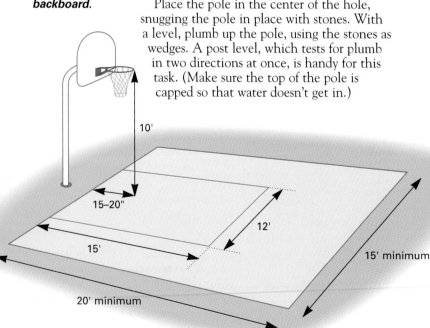

10'

15–20"

15'

12'

15' minimum

20' minimum

CONCRETE WALK

A walk is usually easier to build than a patio because you can reach its entire surface from outside the forms. The techniques for pouring and finishing concrete are the same, but expect differences when laying out the walk and building forms. Because they receive only foot traffic, sidewalks are often just 3 inches thick. In areas without frost heave, you can pour them directly on the ground without a gravel base.

LAYING OUT: Two people can walk together comfortably on a 4-foot-wide walk and can easily pass each other on a 3-foot-wide walk. A person in a wheelchair needs a 40-inch-wide walk, and a person using a walker needs one at least 27 inches wide.

To lay out the walk, stretch two parallel lines between stakes driven into the ground, making sure the walk is square with the house or other predominant features in the landscape. For a curved walk, lay two hoses in the desired shape. Measure between them every foot or so to ensure that each side conforms to the other. Mark the location of the lines or hose with flour, sand, or chalk; then remove them. The surface of the walk should be slightly higher ($\frac{1}{2}$ to 1 inch) than ground level and slightly sloped so water won't puddle.

Excavate the walk the same as you would for a slab (see page 30). Dig to the combined depth of the concrete and gravel base.

MAKING FORMS: Build forms out of 2×4s and stakes. On irregular ground or small slopes, raise or lower the forms to roughly follow the contour of the ground. If the walk slopes more than 1 inch per foot, build stairs or a stepped-down walkway.

All steps should be of equal height and an equal distance apart so that you don't have to adjust your stride as you walk. The easiest way to make a step is to work up the slope. As you build the forms along the sides of the walk and come to a spot needing a step, lay a 2×4 or 2×6 perpendicular to the forms, overlapping the forms about 2 feet. Then continue building forms at this upper level (see the stepped footing on page 27). This crosspiece can be temporary or permanent.

POURING AND FINISHING: Wet the form boards, then pour the concrete and screed it level with the tops of the forms (see pages 34–35). Float the surface and cut control joints with a jointer (see page 36). Space them at intervals equal to $1\frac{1}{2}$ times the width of the walk. Finish the concrete with a broom (see pages 36–37) for a nonslip surface.

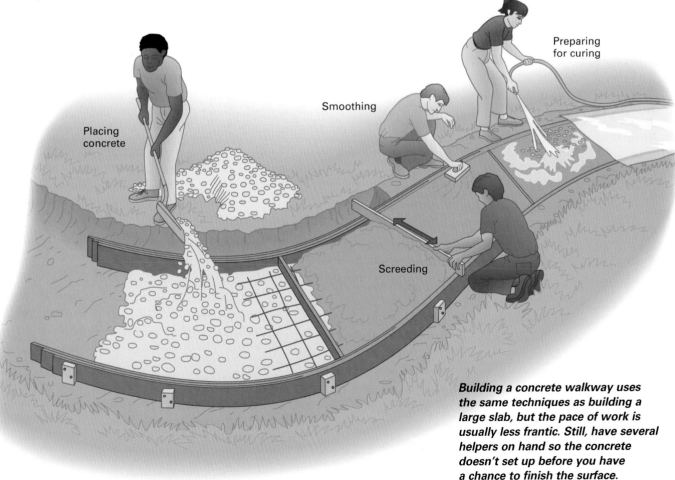

Placing concrete

Smoothing

Preparing for curing

Screeding

Building a concrete walkway uses the same techniques as building a large slab, but the pace of work is usually less frantic. Still, have several helpers on hand so the concrete doesn't set up before you have a chance to finish the surface.

BUILDING CONCRETE STEPS

Steps bridge the gap between our homes and the ground. In the landscape, they link differing grade elevations. The easiest installation is to use precast concrete steps. Typically, these have 6- to 7¼-inch risers (a rise is the height you raise your foot) and 11- to 60-inch-deep runs (a run is the depth of the tread you step on). Landings of precast stairs vary from 4 to 6 feet wide and 30 to 60 inches deep. If your site requires wider landings, shallower risers, or deeper treads—or if you simply like challenges—here's how to build your own steps.

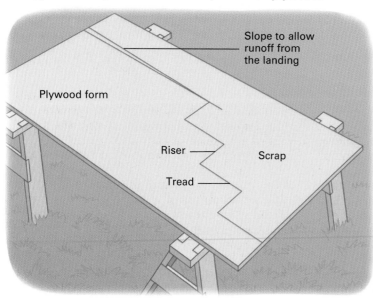

Height of total rise, less thickness of threshold

Above: Find total rise by holding a level 2×4 over the area for the stairs, then measure the distance between the 2×4 and the bottom landing. Excavate deep enough to leave room for the gravel base, the concrete, and any paving you'll use. Also dig holes for piers to support the steps. Below: Draw step forms on plywood.

Slope to allow runoff from the landing

Plywood form

Riser

Tread

Scrap

In the landscape, deep treads and low risers are adequate for gentle slopes. For steep slopes or for access to a standard entry porch, build steps to the dimensions of conventional stairs.

The perception of comfort while climbing steps results from having a correct rise and run. Steps with treads that are too narrow or too deep or with risers that are too tall or too short feel awkward. They can also be dangerous.

Building codes for interior steps typically require 7½-inch-high risers and 11-inch-deep treads. Steps in the landscape tend to be more spacious with a more gradual rise. They can have a run of about 12 to 15 inches for every 6 inches of rise. As a rule, for the most comfort, the total of the tread depth plus the riser height should equal 18 to 22 inches.

When building a set of steps between two fixed heights, such as between a house and a patio, carefully calculate the total rise. This helps ensure each step will be the same height.

To determine total rise, hold a long 2×4 or straightedge level so that one end rests on the upper landing and the other end is suspended above the lower landing (*see the illustration at left*). Measure the distance between the

CASUAL STEPS FOR A SLOPING YARD

For steps that don't need to begin and end at precise points, such as steps in a landscape, use this technique: Dig two 3- to 4-inch-deep trenches in the slope where you want the steps. The trenches should be as far apart as the width of the steps. Set 2×12s on edge in the trenches. Ensure that they are parallel, then stake them in place.

Excavate a series of stepped platforms between the forms. These don't have to conform to the finished steps, they simply provide a place for the 4-inch-thick layer of concrete.

Use plywood for the forms, drawing the stair layout on the plywood sheet. First, mark the point where the steps and the finished surface of the walk leading up to them will meet. Next, using a level, draw the risers and treads, starting at this bottom step and working up. Make light, erasable lines because you'll likely have to experiment before coming up with identical, easy-to-climb steps.

bottom of the straightedge and the lower landing surface. That's the total rise.

Divide this figure by a trial riser height, such as 7 inches. This tells you how many steps to build between the top and bottom landings. Round up the result to the nearest whole number and divide the total rise by that number. You now have the precise riser height for each step.

For example, say the total rise is 55 inches. Divide 55 by a 7-inch trial riser. The result, 8, tells you that it will take eight steps between the lower and upper landings. Next, divide 55 by 8. Now you know that the eight steps will each have a rise of 6.875 inches.

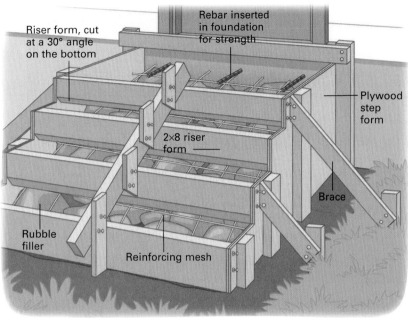

BUILDING FORMS

Excavate the footing deep enough to allow room for a firm gravel base and the thickness of any paving materials, such as brick. Where winters are cold, also dig pier holes that extend below the frost line under each step for extra support.

For steps between fixed heights, cut the form from a sheet of ¾-inch plywood. (You may need two sheets for a large stairway.) Draw the steps on the plywood to the dimensions you calculated earlier, sloping the upper landing so that water drains away from the structure. If the steps will be paved, subtract the thickness of both the paving and bedding material from the height of the first riser only. *Note: All of the other steps should be the height you computed earlier. Keep in mind that the finished surface of the steps will be higher than the tread line on the form.*

Cut the plywood sheet and set it in place to make sure you drew the layout correctly. If it's OK, use this form as a template to mark and cut a sheet for the other side of the stairs. Set the two forms in place and support them with stakes and braces made of 2×4s (*see the illustrations at right*). Check for square and plumb as you assemble the form.

To make forms for the risers, rip-cut 2×8s to the calculated riser height. Cut each of the bottom edges at a 30-degree bevel to leave a space so you can slip a trowel under the form as you finish the step below.

POURING AND FINISHING

Pack gravel into the base of the form, filling the excavation to the bottom of the form. To cut down on the amount of concrete needed, fill the forms with rubble, such as broken pieces of concrete. Leave enough room that the concrete is at least 4 inches thick at all points.

Keep forms upright and plumb with 2×4 stakes and braces. Attach the riser forms to both of the side forms and to step braces to prevent the concrete from deforming the forms.

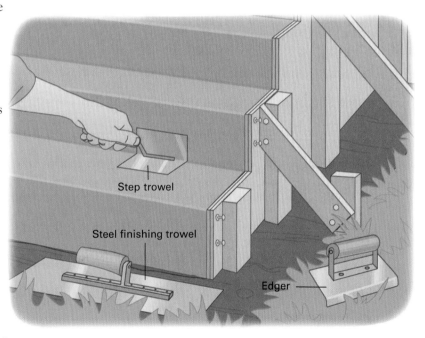

Reinforce the steps with wire mesh. If the steps attach to a house, add strength by inserting rebar into holes drilled in the foundation. Also lay an expansion strip against the foundation to prevent the foundation from cracking.

Starting at the bottom step and working up, pour the concrete flush with the tops of the forms, then screed and trowel. Remove the riser forms when the concrete is firm. Then use a step trowel to finish inside corners, and an edger and a steel trowel for the rest of the step. Cover the steps or keep them moist for five days, then remove the forms.

Finish the inside corner of the step with a step trowel. Its 90-degree angle matches the bend in the step. Rounding the outside edges of the step with an edger prevents chipping.

BRICK, STONE, & TILE PATIOS

A concrete slab provides a functional and durable patio surface. You can dress it up with masonry or build a patio from masonry units alone. Masonry offers a more aesthetic setting for relaxing and entertaining. Although a masonry patio may not be as strong as a concrete slab, it can last for decades and is easier to repair than concrete. And it is easier to build.

Paving brick, flagstone, tile, and natural-looking concrete pavers harmonize with nearly any house exterior. Often, different types of masonry materials mix and match nicely. However, avoid clashing styles: A tight and stately tile surface may look awkward against casual-looking materials such as flagstone or landscaping timbers.

The most common place for a patio is alongside the back of a house. If it is within easy reach of the kitchen, you have a delightful outdoor dining area. Barbecuing and entertaining will be a breeze. Such a patio makes for a graceful transition between the house and the yard: an attractive, usable surface open to the natural world. Include plants in your patio design, either by leaving spaces in which to grow them or by placing generous-sized flower pots around the patio.

This chapter has directions for building all the basic brick, stone, and tile patio options. The simplest construction method is to lay flagstone directly on top of well-tamped soil. To build a sand-laid patio, excavate and set the pavers in a bed of smoothed sand. For a rock-solid patio surface, pour a concrete slab and set bricks or tiles in mortar on top of it. If you have an existing concrete patio in decent shape, you can tile over it as well. Any of these methods will produce a lasting patio surface if you take care to provide a solid subsurface for your patio materials.

Lay out a patio as you would a concrete slab; see pages 16–17 for the basics of layout, and pages 30–32 for instructions on excavating and tamping. A masonry patio built in an area subject to frost can be built without a footing and allowed to "float"—rise and fall when the ground freezes and thaws. Excavate by hand or with a small earth-moving machine. In most cases, it is easiest to remove the sod, then install the edging material. Attach taut string lines to the edging for use as depth guides as you finish the excavation.

AVOID BACK STRAIN

Although you might never pick up very heavy objects while building a patio, the cumulative effect of working with brick and stone can damage your back. Hours spent on your knees moving bricks may not feel like hard work while you're doing it, but it is not unusual for a do-it-yourselfer to wind up with a severely strained lower back. So take it easy.

In addition to being a long-lasting, easily maintained surface, a masonry patio blends beautifully with plantings and the surrounding landscape.

DESIGNING AND PLANNING A PATIO

Take your time when planning a patio. A structure this permanent is well worth several weekends of planning, multiple trips to brickyards, and a couple of on-site family meetings.

Don't limit yourself to home centers and lumberyards when choosing materials. Many brickyards cater to the public as well as to professionals (call them if you are not sure). They may carry a wealth of paving materials that you won't find anywhere else.

Tailor the design of the patio to your yard. For example, the area beneath a large tree whose shade inhibits lawn growth might be the perfect spot for a small, dry-laid brick patio. Instead of a standard rectangular brick pattern, consider a circular or curving design that emphasizes the shape of the tree. This same treatment works well for patios in other areas of the yard that have a central focal point, such as a seating area or pond.

PAVING PATTERNS

All the paving patterns illustrated below will form strong patios. As long as the bricks or pavers are placed tightly together and the joint lines are filled completely with sand, they will resist buckling just as well as interlocking pavers with complicated shapes.

Choose the pattern that is most pleasing to your eye.

If you use the running bond or herringbone pattern, you will have to cut some bricks when you come to the edge. The other patterns form squares, so you can avoid cutting bricks, as long as you can move the edging when you come to the end.

Don't shy away from unusual patterns. For instance, it's fairly easy to make curves. Many pavers are manufactured to go together to form curved shapes. Pavers for circular designs come in several shapes, which allow you to start with a center piece and work outward without having to make complicated cuts. Ask your supplier for suggestions.

EDGINGS: Patio materials—especially those set in sand—need to be encased in a frame so they won't drift or loosen. Choose an edging that matches the pavers in appearance or strikes a pleasing contrast. In most cases, the edging should extend more deeply into the ground than the paving materials to provide stability for both the edging and the patio.

Install the edging before the pavers, and plan the excavation so the top of the edging is flush with or slightly lower than the top of the paver surface. For information on edging techniques, see pages 48–49.

FORMED CONCRETE EDGING: This is the strongest type of edging. It is not attractive by itself, but you can cover it with brick or tile.

Running bond

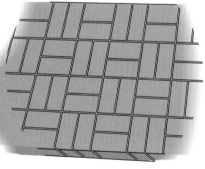

Basket weave

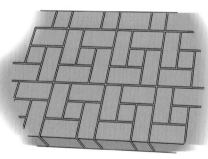

Pinwheel

Half-basket weave

BRICK PATTERNS

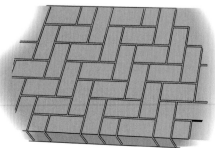

Herringbone 90°

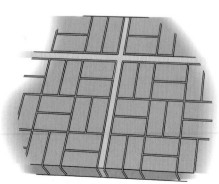

Grid pattern

BRICK "SOLDIERS": These are single bricks you simply set upright or diagonally in the ground with soil or sand tamped around them. To ensure that they won't move, set them in a bed of concrete, then pack in soil or sand.

LANDSCAPING TIMBERS: Edging timbers, such as railroad ties or 4×4s, provide a pleasing contrast to bricks or concrete. Smaller pieces of lumber, such as 2×4s, can also be used, but you must stake them every couple of feet and firmly backfill them with tamped soil.

MANUFACTURED EDGINGS: Steel edging makes quick work of curves. Bend it into position and drive metal stakes into the ground to hold it in place. Plastic edging is also easy, but low-end lines of plastic edging may not hold up over time.

PATIO DRAINAGE

Think through drainage carefully to avoid puddles on the patio or the lawn. Slope the patio away from the house so water will run off easily. Not much will drain through the cracks—even if the pavers are set in sand. A patio should slope at a rate of 1 inch per 10 running feet.

If the patio will be near the end of a downspout, extend the downspout away from the house. Or tie it into an underground drainpipe. Here's how: Dig a trench across the patio excavation and place flexible drainpipe in the trench; connect the downspout to the drainpipe.

If this solution proves impractical, dig a dry well. This is a hole 4 feet wide and 4 feet deep, filled with rock or gravel. Extend the downspout to the dry well, cover the extension with 3 to 4 inches of gravel, and backfill with topsoil.

If water puddles around the perimeter of a patio, make a French drain: Trench around the patio, then pour gravel into the trench. Mulched shrub and flower beds with loosened or well-amended sandy or loamy soil may also offer a quick fix.

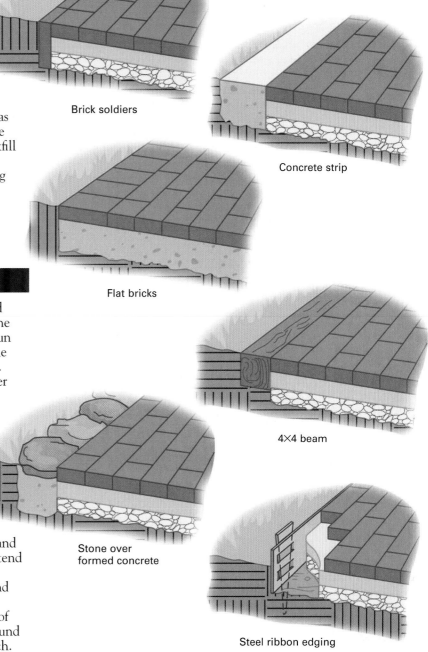

EDGINGS

Brick soldiers

Concrete strip

Flat bricks

4×4 beam

Stone over formed concrete

Steel ribbon edging

2×4 on edge

Standing wood trim

Edging keeps the pavers from wandering while it provides pleasing visual contrast as well. Some of the more common types of edgings are shown here. Use your imagination to improvise others.

SETTING BRICKS OR PAVERS IN SAND

Laying bricks or pavers in a smooth bed of sand is a fairly quick and easy way to install a patio, a walk—even a driveway. This technique allows you to work in easy stages, leaving the job partly finished and picking it up later—something you cannot do when working with concrete or mortar. The keys to success are a well-compacted base and a firm edging around the perimeter.

Use the methods on pages 16–17 to lay out the mason's lines before you begin; see pages 30–31 for tips on excavation. Plan to tamp both the soil and the gravel so that the patio won't develop waves after a few years.

INSTALL EDGING FIRST

It is usually easiest to install the edging first so you can use it as a guide for excavating soil, screeding sand, and laying bricks.

To minimize how many bricks or pavers you have to cut, install edging on two adjacent sides only. Start your brickwork at the permanent edgings and move outward. When you reach the end, install the other edging pieces tight against the bricks. With the running bond and herringbone patterns (see page 46), you'll still need to cut some bricks.

ABOVEGROUND EDGING: If the patio will sit 2 inches or more above the surrounding grade, a good choice for edging is 4×4, 6×6, or 8×8 landscaping timbers. Use wood that is guaranteed not to rot, such as pressure-treated lumber marked "ground contact." Select straight pieces.

Set the timbers on a bed of tamped gravel, butting their ends. Toenail them together with galvanized 5-inch nails. Drill holes every 4 feet or so, then drive 3-foot lengths of rebar or galvanized pipe through the timber and into the ground.

FLUSH EDGING: Edging that is nearly flush with the ground can be made quickly and inexpensively from redwood or pressure-treated 2×4s. Dig a trench about 6 inches below the level of the patio surface and 3 inches wide. Shovel 2½ inches of gravel into the trench, tamp, and set the boards in it at the correct height. Support them with 12-inch 1×2 stakes, driven every 4 feet and nailed to the outside of the boards. As you work, make sure that the tops of the stakes are an inch or so below the tops of the edging boards.

To install upright "soldiers," dig an edging trench and add enough sand so you can set the bricks at the desired height; use a string line to keep them straight. Tap the soldiers in with a hammer and board. Backfill the row with soil and tamp lightly. After you install the patio surface, tamp the backfilled soil firmly, adding more soil as needed.

To make a formed concrete edging, install 2×4 forms to the height of the layout lines. Dig a trench at least 4 inches wide, and deep enough for 2 to 3 inches of tamped gravel topped off with 4 inches of concrete.

Using a vibrating compactor will ensure that the sand rests on firm soil and/or gravel. Inadequate tamping can cause unsightly dips in the patio surface after a year or two.

Set upright brick "soldiers" in a level trench lined with 2 inches of gravel or sand. Gently tamp dirt or sand around them.

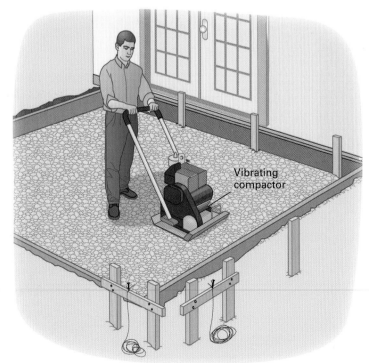

Vibrating compactor

EXCAVATE THE SITE

With the edging in place, remove all organic material—sod and any roots thicker than ½ inch—from the patio bed. Dig the area to a level depth equal to the pavers' thickness plus 2 inches. If the ground is wet for much of the year, which may cause the completed brickwork to settle unevenly, excavate at least an extra 2 inches so you can place gravel under the sand.

After excavating, tamp the soil. You can make a tamping tool from a 6-foot length of 4×4 attached to a 10-inch-square plywood plate. Better yet, use a vibrating compactor. The compactor is heavy, so enlist a helper to move it to the site. As the compactor starts, it may feel as though it's taking off; once you've got the hang of how it handles, make several passes. Fill in any depressions and compact the area again.

Order gravel and sand, and schedule their delivery so they can be dumped directly into the patio area. To estimate how many cubic yards you will need, multiply the thickness in feet (for instance, 4 inches = 0.33 feet) times the width (in feet) times the length of the patio (in feet), then divide the result by 27 to get cubic yards. Spread the gravel and tamp it.

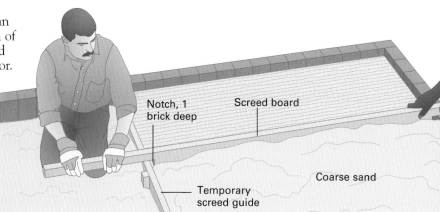

For a large patio, work in sections. Install a temporary screed guide. Rest the screed on the guide and on the edging to screed the first section.

THE SAND BASE

For the sand base, order unwashed coarse sand. It is less expensive than washed fine sand and works just as well. Using a shovel and wheelbarrow, spread sand in the patio area.

Make a screed board by notch-cutting the ends of a straight 2×4 to produce "ears" that are a foot or more long. It should screed the sand to a depth of a paver's thickness below the top of the edging.

Place the screed on the edging, and draw it across the sand, working it back and forth in a sawing motion as you pull it toward you. If the patio is too wide for the screed to reach across it, install a temporary guide by staking and leveling a 2×4 down the center of the patio site. Dampen the sand to compact it, spread a thin layer of sand on top, and screed again to provide a firm, smooth base for laying the bricks or pavers.

Before arranging the bricks or pavers, you may want to place landscaping fabric over the sand. This fabric allows water to penetrate but inhibits weed growth. The fabric also prevents ridges of sand from working up between the bricks as you place them.

Install the pavers for the first section, using string stretched between the edging and the temporary screed as a height guide.

Remove the temporary guide, and screed the next section.

SETTING BRICKS OR PAVERS IN SAND

continued

PLACING THE BRICKS OR PAVERS

Starting at one corner, lay the bricks or pavers in your selected pattern. Place them firmly on the sand or landscape fabric, leaving a space of 1/8 inch or less between them. Avoid sliding them into place so as to keep the sand surface smooth and level. To distribute your weight and to keep from pushing individual bricks or pavers out of place as you work, kneel on a half sheet of plywood or a few boards on top of the bricks.

You may need to brush in sand and spray with water several times before the joints are completely filled.

To settle the bricks, tap them lightly with a hammer handle or rubber mallet. Or simply set them, then go over them later with a power compactor. Every three or four rows, check the joints for straightness, using a mason's line.

After seating the bricks, sprinkle a thin layer of fine, dry sand over the bricks. With a broom, sweep it gently back and forth to work the grains of sand into the joints. You're not doing this simply to make a pleasing appearance: The grains of sand act as tiny

CUTTING BRICKS OR PAVERS

To work efficiently when cutting bricks, do them all at once. Complete the installation of the patio or walk, leaving only the spaces that require cut bricks. To mark bricks for cutting, hold a full brick flush against the edging and over a set brick. The brick you're holding should be level and not dip at any point. With a pencil, mark the overlap of the brick you're holding on the set brick. Swap a full brick for the marked brick, then cut the marked brick along the scribe line. Now, this brick will fit the gap between the full brick and the edging.

wedges to keep the bricks from moving. (When hosing off the patio or walk later, take care to not hose out the sand.)

Finish up by settling the bricks and sand with a power compactor, or spray the patio surface with a fine mist of water and let it dry. Repeat until the sand works its way fully into the joints.

BUILDING A BRICK-ON-SAND SIDEWALK

For one person to stroll comfortably, a sidewalk needs to be 3 feet wide; 4 feet is wide enough for two people to walk side-by-side. Begin construction by installing a strip of steel edging or redwood benderboard to follow your layout lines. Next, pour in the sand and level it. Cut the bottom of the screed in a curve so that it forms a crown in the middle of the sand bed; this ensures that water runs off to either side. Compact the sand, screed it, and compact again. Lay the bricks along the entire length of the walk, then install the second edging strip tight to the bricks.

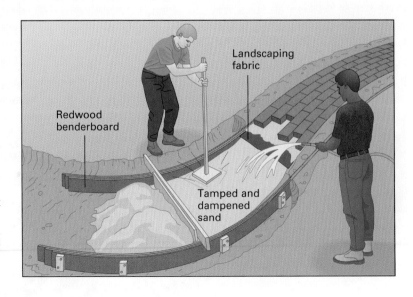

Landscaping fabric

Redwood benderboard

Tamped and dampened sand

STONE WALKS

A stone walk through a garden or across a lawn is a classic feature that is easy to build. Install stepping-stone walks in places that receive light foot traffic. Select stones that are large, flat, and similar in size, or buy precast concrete stepping-stones.

STEPPING-STONE PATH

Establish the general outline and location of the walk by laying two parallel lengths of hose or rope on the ground. Using the hose as a guide, lay out the stones. You may be tempted to use a random spacing, but regular spacings will make for easier walking. Test for comfort by strolling on the stones. They should match your stride, neither so close you have to tiptoe nor so far apart you have to stretch.

Once you have established the positions of all the stones, cut the outline of each individual stone in the sod with a shovel or spade. Set the stone off to the side, remove the sod, and excavate its space so the stone will sit slightly above grade but low enough to run the lawn mower across it.

Tamp the soil with a piece of 4×4, then set the stone back in place. You will probably need to make adjustments, removing or adding dirt under the stone and packing it until the stone is seated firmly. Repeat with all the stones. You may have to reset a few of the stones every few years.

Cut sod, using stone as guide.

Fill low spots under flagstone until level.

USING CONTRASTING GRAVEL

Many landscape architects favor the technique of building walks with large flagstones in a bed of crushed rock or rounded, light-colored pebbles. Lay out the walk as you would a regular stepping-stone path, marking its edges about a foot beyond the flagstones. (The width of the path depends on the scale you want to achieve, as well as the size of the crushed rock or pebbles you are using.)

Dig a trench for the edging, and remove all sod and organic matter from the path area. Apply a preemergence weed killer (loose stones may not prevent weed growth), then lay down landscaping fabric.

Install the edging and backfill it. Place crushed stone or pebbles between the edges of the path, and screed so that it is 1 to 2 inches below the edging.

Set the flagstones flush with the top of the edging. You may have to add or remove crushed stone or pebbles beneath them to ensure they are firmly seated and don't wobble. When the flagstones are set, add stone or pebbles so they are nearly flush with the top of the flagstones.

Determine the contours of a stepping-stone path by laying two parallel hoses on the ground. Give it a test walk before permanently setting stones in the ground.

A stepping-stone path is an easy project that you can finish in a weekend. Set stones a comfortable stride apart, taking care to level them so they won't tip when trod upon.

DRY-SET FLAGSTONE

Flagstone is ideal for making a handsome informal patio or walkway surface that will suit almost any style of architecture. With its irregular shape and size, flagstone is versatile and appealing. However, it is bumpy, which can make walking and scooting furniture around on it a bit difficult.

You can lay flagstone in mortar (*see pages 54–56*) or in sand. Even simpler is setting it on well-tamped soil and filling the cracks with more soil. However, grass or moss will grow in the cracks, and you will probably need to reset some stones every few years.

PREPARING THE GROUND: Lay out the site with rope or a hose. Plan to slope the patio away from the house. Although some rainwater will seep between the cracks, not all of it will.

Remove the sod and any roots thicker than ½ inch. Rake the soil surface, then firm it with a power tamper (especially if you are dealing with a large area) or a hand-tamper. Fill in any low spots and retamp.

Finish by scattering ½ inch of soil over the site and raking it lightly. The soil helps to firmly seat the stones. Because the finished patio should be ½ inch or more above the surrounding ground, you may need to add more than ½ inch of soil. Install edging (*see pages 46 and 48*), or use larger stones around the perimeter.

LAYING THE STONES: Order 10 percent more stones than will fill your patio area to allow for waste. When the stones arrive, you'll notice that they are of various sizes. Separate them into piles according to size, and systematically choose from the piles so that you evenly distribute the various sizes over the surface. Don't neglect this step. If an area has all small or all large stones, the work looks amateurish.

Take time setting the stones in place. You'll probably need to try several arrangements until you are pleased with the pattern. Aim for joint lines that don't vary greatly in width.

Use uncut stones as much as possible. Occasionally you will need to cut a stone, especially if the patio has edging. Use an adjoining stone as a template: Set it on top of the stone to be cut, then trace around it. Score the line by tapping with a hammer and brickset. Then place the stone over a 2×2 or a length of pipe, and strike sharply on the scored line with the hammer and brickset.

Remove all sod and organic matter. Rake the area to level the area, then tamp it firm. Finally, scatter ½ inch or so of soil over the area, and rake lightly.

Experiment with flagstones until you find a pattern with joint lines of fairly consistent width. Use a variety of sizes so you don't end up with a lot of little stones in one area.

Another way to score the cut line is to use a circular saw equipped with a masonry blade. Be sure to wear a dust mask, gloves, and protective eyewear.

Once the stones are in place, test each one to be certain it is firmly bedded. Any wobbling now won't disappear in time. Stand on the stone to leave an impression in the soil, which will tell you where to scrape away and where to fill. Expect to make two or three attempts before each stone is firmly and evenly set.

FILLING THE JOINTS: If you will plant between the stones, carefully shovel soil into the joints; otherwise, you can use sand. Wet the soil with a fine mist to settle it into the joints. Add more soil, then spray again; repeat until the soil is just below the stone surface.

A nursery can recommend plants to use between stones. Hardy ground covers, such as creeping thyme, are popular. Keep weeds out of joints; their deep roots can buckle the patio.

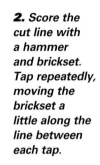

CUTTING FLAGSTONE

1. **Place an adjoining stone on top, and trace a cut line.**

2. **Score the cut line with a hammer and brickset. Tap repeatedly, moving the brickset a little along the line between each tap.**

3. **Set the stone on a pipe, place the brickset on the score, then break the stone with a single strong blow.**

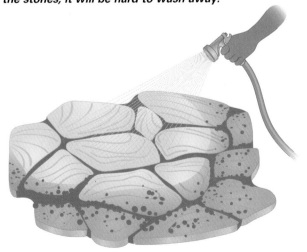

Take care not to step on soil that has spilled onto the stones; it will be hard to wash away.

Use a hose with the nozzle set on "fine spray" or "mist" to simultaneously clean the stones and soak the soil in the joints.

SAND-LAID FLAGSTONE

Building a sand-laid flagstone patio is much like building a sand-laid brick or paver patio. (*See pages 48–50 for instructions on excavating, tamping, and screeding.*) The patio will need a solid edging to keep the sand from leaking out.

If you don't want plants to grow between the stones, lay landscaping fabric *before* you pour the sand. (You can't put the fabric on top of the sand as you can for a brick patio, because flagstones have irregular surfaces.) Depending on your climate, you may need to apply herbicide several times a year. Some sand will come out of the cracks as you use the patio, but light sweeping will keep the problem under control.

Install the edging, and set the perimeter first, using stones with one straight side so they fit fairly tight against the edging. Then work inward to arrange the remaining stones.

Setting stones in sand is a bit easier than setting them in soil. Keep the sand moist as you work. You can often take out small wobbles by pushing down on a stone and twisting it into place. Take extra care to see that the stones are flush with each other and form a fairly level surface. Repeatedly mist and sweep the sand into the joints until the joint sand is firm. Expect to add more sand every couple of years; rain will slowly wash it away.

TILING OVER A CONCRETE SLAB

If you have a concrete slab in place and it's reasonably solid, then mortaring bricks, tile, or stone over it will be easier than tearing up the old slab and installing a sand-laid patio. If you will be paving with tiles, be sure they are strong enough for use as an outside patio surface. Glazed tiles will be slippery; quarry tiles are a good choice.

To lay an isolation membrane, spread it with the notched side of the trowel, then remove the ridges using the flat side of the trowel.

PREPARE THE CONCRETE SLAB

NEW SLAB: To lay a new slab, follow the directions on pages 30–37. Keep in mind that you'll need to excavate to a depth that includes the thickness of the brick or tiles. Don't expect the paving material to add much strength; be sure to construct the slab according to local codes. You don't need to finish the concrete, but tiling over it will be easier if you at least smooth it with a magnesium float.

EXISTING SLAB: When working with an existing slab, use a long, straight board to test for level. If the patio has any high spots, use a brickset and baby sledge to knock them down. Fill low spots with patching concrete. If areas are loose and wobbly, chip them out, then refill them with fresh concrete mix. If the surface is flaking, scrape and remove all loose materials.

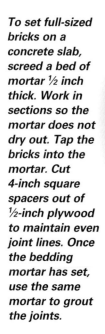

LAY AN ISOLATION MEMBRANE:
Isolation membranes are important when installing tile over a concrete slab. Placed atop the slab, they keep the tile and grout from cracking as the slab swells and contracts with the seasons. Apply the membrane with the notched side of a tiling trowel to ensure a good bond. Then smooth it with the flat side of the trowel. Work using long, sweeping strokes. Let the membrane cure completely.

LAY OUT THE JOB

To lay irregular stones, arrange them on the slab, following the directions on pages 52–53. Once you have the pattern you like, you will pick up only a few stones at a time (keeping track of where they go), spread mortar, and set them back in place.

For square or rectangular tiles or pavers, draw two perpendicular layout lines near the center of the job (*see page 55*). You will start laying tiles against these lines. The idea is to plan so the last row isn't made up of tile slivers or of tiles that increase in size along the length of the slab. A quick way to draw layout lines is to trace along the corner of a sheet of plywood.

The safest way to measure is to dry-lay the units on the slab, complete with spacers. This actually doesn't take much time, and it is a good prevention against layout mistakes. Be sure you know how each edge will look all along its length.

To set full-sized bricks on a concrete slab, screed a bed of mortar ½ inch thick. Work in sections so the mortar does not dry out. Tap the bricks into the mortar. Cut 4-inch square spacers out of ½-inch plywood to maintain even joint lines. Once the bedding mortar has set, use the same mortar to grout the joints.

Don't place so much mortar that it will set before the bricks can be laid.

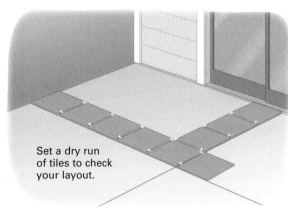

Set a dry run of tiles to check your layout.

Draw perpendicular layout lines near the middle of the job, and set the tiles in a dry run—complete with spacers—to make sure you will not end up with slivers or a row of tiles that noticeably grows larger along its length.

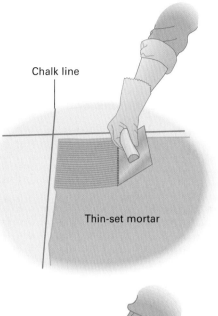

Using a notched trowel, spread thin-set mortar over a small area so that you will have time to lay all the tiles before the thin-set sets up. Avoid covering layout lines.

Chalk line

Thin-set mortar

SETTING TILES

Use thin-set mortar (a mortar for ceramic tiles) mixed with liquid latex additive—it is stronger than water-mixed thin-set. In a 5-gallon bucket, mix only as much thin-set as you can use in half an hour. If you have a lot of mixing to do, use a drill with a $\frac{1}{2}$-inch chuck equipped with a mixing blade. Mix thoroughly, let the thin-set rest for 10 minutes, then mix it again. Work in sections small enough that you can lay all the tiles in 10 minutes. If you try to do too large of an area, your mortar will begin to set before you can finish.

Depending on the size of the tile, use a trowel with $\frac{1}{4}$-inch by $\frac{1}{4}$-inch or $\frac{3}{4}$-inch by $\frac{3}{8}$-inch notches. Apply the mortar first with the flat side of the trowel, then rake it level with the notched side. Gently sweep the trowel across the mortar, using long, arcing strokes. The notches shouldn't go so deep as to scrape the slab.

When installing tiles, use spacers to keep joints even. Drop each tile in place, then give it a slight twist to ensure the thin-set adheres at all points. Tap each unit with a hammer and beater block made of a scrap piece of 2×6 wrapped with carpet. Stand back every few minutes and eyeball the joints carefully. Quickly make any adjustments to each section before the mortar starts to set.

Cut tiles as you go, or install all the full tiles, wait for them to set, then cut and install all the edge and corner pieces. To make straight cuts in tiles, use a snap cutter. For cuts that go in two or three directions, use a wet saw. Many home centers will make these cuts for a small fee.

Beater block

Firmly embed the tile in the mortar by tapping it with a beater block. Make a block by stapling a scrap of carpeting to a 2×4 scrap. This also ensures that adjacent units are at the same height.

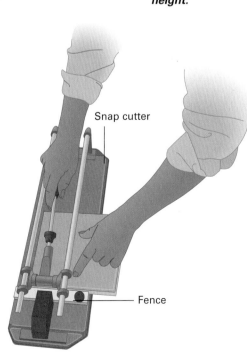

Use a snap cutter for all straight cuts. Set the tile firmly against the fence; drag the cutting wheel across the tile in one smooth stroke to scribe a line on the tile. Push down on the handle to snap the cut along the line.

Snap cutter

Fence

TILING OVER A CONCRETE SLAB
continued

Use sweeping, diagonal strokes—both to push the grout into the joints and to scrape away the excess. Look for a grout float with a smooth rubber face, backed by foam rubber; it will work better than one with a permeable, foam-rubber surface.

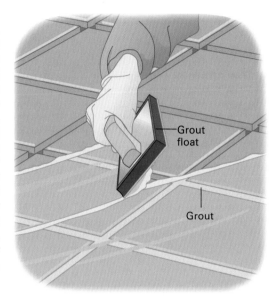

Grout float

Grout

GROUT AND CLEAN

Let the mortar set completely for a day or two. Pry the spacers out with small screwdriver. Scrape away mortar that is on the tiles or that sticks up in the joints.

Mix sanded grout (made for floor tiles) with latex additive, and apply it with a laminated grout float. First push the grout into the joints, holding the float nearly flat and moving it in at least two diagonal directions at all points. Before the surface has a chance to dry, tilt the float at a 45-degree angle to squeegee away excess.

Within a half hour, clean the tiles, first by laying a wet towel on the surface and dragging it, then by wiping with a sponge. Rinse the sponge repeatedly. Work carefully so all the joints are consistent in depth and appearance. Rinse at least twice. Allow the surface to dry, then buff the tiles with a dry cloth.

LAYING FLAGSTONES ON CONCRETE

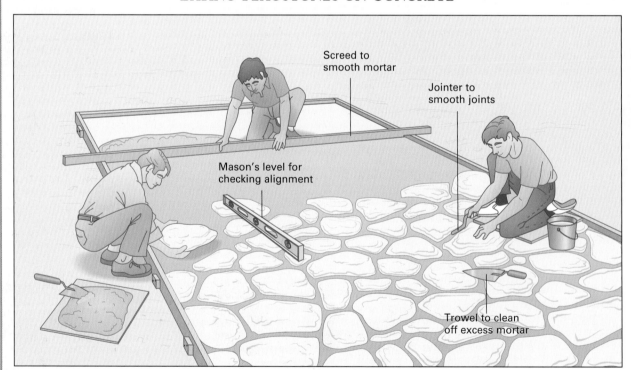

Screed to smooth mortar

Jointer to smooth joints

Mason's level for checking alignment

Trowel to clean off excess mortar

Before mixing mortar, set a large section of the stones in place on the slab; see pages 52–53 for tips on arranging and cutting them. Mix 1 part portland cement with 3 parts sand. It should be a stiff mixture so the stones won't sink down into it. Remove a few stones and set them to the side; be sure you remember where each goes. Spread the mortar about an inch thick, and place the stones back into it. Tap each stone lightly to bed it. Use a level or a straight board to keep the tops of adjacent stones even. Allow the mortar to cure slowly. Cover it with plastic for about four days to keep it from drying out.

ASPHALT

If you're looking for an inexpensive, easy paving alternative, asphalt may be it. Don't try laying asphalt yourself; the job calls for special heavy-duty equipment. An asphalt company can install a driveway in a day for much less than pouring a concrete slab. Hire a company that has been around for a while and can back up their guarantee.

Also called blacktop or macadam, asphalt is essentially a mixture of sand, gravel, and petroleum products. Asphalt is flexible and fairly soft. It is much easier to install and repair than concrete, but it also requires regular maintenance. Roots can lift and crack asphalt more readily than concrete, so remove all large roots before paving.

A good asphalt crew will work only on a warm day, when the asphalt can be properly compacted. They will bring the asphalt to the site already heated, rather than heating it on site. For a standard driveway, they should first lay 6 to 8 inches of gravel and then run a rolling compactor over it until the gravel is nearly rock-hard. They will then pour and roll 2 to 3 inches of asphalt.

A very strong surface is made by laying a 2-inch-thick layer, rolling it completely, then laying and rolling a second 2-inch-thick layer. Simply laying a single 3-inch or thicker layer will not result in an adequately compacted and thus strong driveway.

The crew should leave behind a completely smooth surface, with no ridges higher than ⅛ inch. A well-rolled surface will be free of small holes, which collect water and produce cracks when the water freezes.

Make sure the driveway is graded so that water runs off where you want it to go. Any puddles that collect on the surface will cause serious damage when they go through the freeze-thaw cycles of winter.

Discuss edging possibilities with the contractor. Some prefer to install a metal border with stakes driven deep into the ground. The most stable edging is a ribbon of concrete, but that can be expensive.

A couple of months after the surface is laid, be sure to apply an asphalt sealer, using a special (but inexpensive) tool that looks like a push broom with a squeegee attachment. Apply this sealer regularly— every couple of years or so—to keep hairline cracks from developing into serious problems.

An asphalt crew that's doing its job right will roll, roll, roll. Each successive layer of gravel and asphalt must be thoroughly compacted.

MASONRY WALLS

There is a certain romantic quality to building with natural stone and brick. The techniques have changed little over many centuries; Egyptians used string lines to align courses while building the pyramids—the same technique we use when building garden walls. Though it may seem frustrating at first, you'll find a special kind of pride in the masonry projects that you complete. And the work itself can be satisfyingly meditative as well.

If you watch a professional mason lay a row of bricks, you could easily get the impression that there is nothing to it—just follow the string line, spread the mortar, and lay one on top of two, two on top of one. But that mason spent years practicing on the job so that throwing mortar and setting bricks have become second nature.

Don't expect to start building large brick or block walls after only a day or two of practice. Start small, work slowly, and build walls that you will point to with pride for years. Some projects, such as a mortarless block wall or an interlocking retaining wall, do not require actual masonry skills. Others, such as a small brick planter or a low stone retaining wall, require concentration and effort but are eminently "doable." And once you have completed them, you may feel emboldened to move on to more aggressive feats of masonry derring-do.

When building a wall with brick or block, it is especially important to start out right. Begin with a level concrete foundation, and take special care that those first masonry units are laid straight, level, and plumb. It will be difficult to correct even a small mistake or misalignment as you build upward.

Many masonry walls—especially stone walls—have a rough-hewn quality to them that may make you think they are sloppily built. But if you look closely, you will find that the courses are actually straight and the joints are consistent. A poorly built wall doesn't look rustic; it looks unprofessional. Follow the instructions in this chapter, and take time to practice. You'll be proud of your results.

Whether of stone or brick, a masonry wall blends beautifully with plantings such as those surrounding this garden pond. In addition, the durability of a masonry wall makes it a landscaping feature well worth the effort.

TOOLS AND TECHNIQUES

Tools for working with brick and stone have changed little over the centuries. For a modest cost, you can assemble a set of good-quality masonry tools. Here's what you'll need.

CHOOSING TOOLS

HAMMERS AND CHISELS:
A *brick* or *mason's hammer* has one head for hammering and another head for cutting and shaping brick. Choose one with a handle made of wood, fiberglass, or steel, with a rubber grip to absorb shock. A *rubber mallet* allows you to tap bricks into place without fear of breaking them. A *brickset* is a wide chisel used for splitting and dressing bricks.

LEVELS:
Any accurate 4-foot level will do. *Mason's levels* are made of brass and wood. Although expensive, they take plenty of abuse and are easier to clean than all-metal levels. A *torpedo level*, which is smaller than a mason's level, is handy for checking short spans. A *line level*, which you hang from a taut string, lets you check for level over long spans.

TROWELS:
Your tool chest should include trowels of various shapes; be sure to keep them clean. A *brick trowel* is designed to lay a bed of mortar. A *pointing trowel* is used to push mortar into narrow joints and then smooth it. A *finishing trowel* is used for preparing surfaces and smoothing mortar caps. *Jointers*, which come in various shapes and sizes, are used to smooth and finish mortar joints.

MARKING TOOLS:
Chalk line quickly marks long, perfectly straight lines. Nylon *mason's line* won't sag while stringing a layout. *Line blocks* help keep courses straight. A steel *framing square* (also called a carpenter's square) enables you to check right angles.

MISCELLANEOUS:
A *brick tong* lets you clamp and carry up to 10 bricks at a time, saving wear and tear on your hands. A *mortarboard* handily holds a shovelful or two of mortar near the working surface. Make one by screwing a 2-foot-square piece of plywood to two 2×4 legs, or purchase a hand-held aluminum board called a hawk. A hawk is handy for small jobs, but you can't set it down without spilling the mortar.

Have a few *brushes* of varying stiffness on hand for cleaning spilled mortar. Wear *safety goggles* whenever cutting or chipping masonry.

In addition to the tools on this page, purchase a *masonry blade* for your circular saw and a *mason's rule*. This is a 6-foot folding rule or retractable steel tape with numbered guides, which you use to check the height of brick and mortar joints. Or, you can check them with a *story pole*. Make one by marking a straight 2×2 with lines at the height of each course of brick in the wall you are building.

Have a 25-foot steel *tape measure* handy for laying out patios, walks, or walls, plus a 100-foot tape measure for larger projects.

Rubber mallet / Brick hammer / Finishing trowel / Brickset / Jointer / Pointing trowel / Brick trowel / Line level / Torpedo level / Mason's level

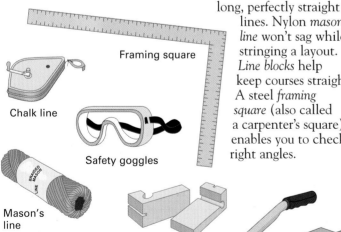
Framing square / Chalk line / Safety goggles / Mason's line

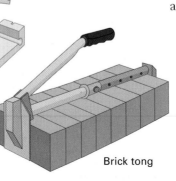
Line blocks / Brush / Brick tong

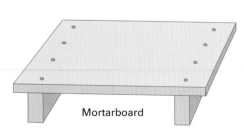
Mortarboard

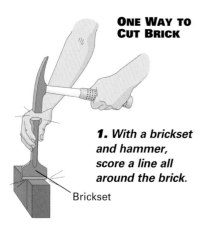

ONE WAY TO CUT BRICK

1. **With a brickset and hammer, score a line all around the brick.**

Brickset

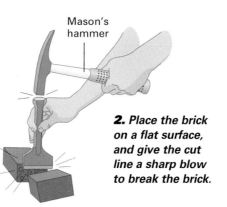

Mason's hammer

2. **Place the brick on a flat surface, and give the cut line a sharp blow to break the brick.**

3. **Chip away large protruding particles with a mason's hammer.**

4. **Smooth the edge further by scraping with a trowel.**

CUTTING BRICK

Many pros can hold a brick with one hand and strike it with the edge of their trowel, and zap!—a cleanly cut brick. Those of us without years of practice won't find brick cutting that easy. Here are three methods.

BRICKSET AND HAMMER: Wear safety goggles as you work. Measure and mark the cutting line on all sides of the brick, then score the brick by tapping a brickset with a hammer along the cutting line. Set the brick on a firm, level surface. Place the brickset on the scored line with its bevel facing the side that will be waste, and strike it with a single forceful blow. Use the chisel end of the mason's hammer to remove protruding chunks, then smooth the edge with a trowel.

CIRCULAR SAW WITH MASONRY BLADE: Some hardened bricks and stone are all but impossible to cut by hand. Use a power saw with a masonry blade. You can use your own circular saw, but such heavy use will wear it out—especially if it's a homeowner-quality

saw. For heavy-duty or repeated cutting, use a gasoline-powered saw (*see page 50*).

It's important to secure the brick before cutting it. Use a vise or a folding worktable with a top that clamps. (C-clamps get in the way of the saw.)

MASONRY SAW: Rent a masonry saw with a table if you have a lot of cutting to do. Set the brick on the table, and align the cutting mark with the saw blade. Start the motor, then gently lower the blade onto the brick. Move the blade back and forth over the brick with a minimum of downward pressure— let the blade do the work. Keep your fingers away from the saw blade. If the saw is the type with a stationary blade and a movable table, slide the table slowly toward the blade until it cuts through the brick.

If the blade doesn't go completely through the brick, turn the brick over and cut from the other side. Don't try to sever it with a hammer blow; doing so leaves a jagged edge.

MIXING MORTAR

For small jobs, buy mortar mix in 60-pound bags and add water. For larger jobs it may save money to make your own from bulk materials, using the proportions of ingredients below. Choose one of these mortar types to meet the job requirements:

■ **Type M:** The highest strength; use for load-bearing walls and wherever masonry will contact the ground.
■ **Type S:** Fairly high strength; for aboveground exterior use.
■ **Type N:** Medium-strength; suitable for freestanding walls.
■ **Type O:** Low-strength mortar; sufficient for interior masonry or where bricks aren't subject to freezing weather.
Mix each type according to the following proportions:

Type	Cement	Lime	Sand
M	1	$\frac{1}{4}$	$3\frac{3}{4}$
S	1	$\frac{1}{2}$	$4\frac{1}{2}$
N	1	1	6
O	1	2	9

PREPARING TO BUILD A BRICK WALL

The next six pages describe techniques for building a freestanding garden wall, a retaining wall, or brick veneer on a house wall. Before starting, see if your local building department has special requirements.

DESIGNING THE WALL

First, some terms: A *stretcher* is a brick laid so its long edge faces out. A *header* is a brick turned so its end faces out. A *course* of bricks is one horizontal row. *Wythe* refers to how many bricks thick a wall is.

Freestanding walls usually need to be double-wythe—two bricks thick. A single stack of bricks can be easily pushed over. For an extra strong wall, build it of concrete block (*see pages 68–70*) and face it with brick.

BOND PATTERNS: Choose among various ways of stacking bricks, called bond patterns. The three shown below will all make strong walls because their joints are staggered; choose the one that pleases you. *Running bond*—"the old one-on-top-of-two"—uses all stretchers except at the ends, where there is a half brick (sometimes called a "header") every other course.

A *Flemish bond* consists of stretchers and headers arranged to align every other course. *English bond* is made by alternating rows of stretchers and headers.

CAPS: If the top of your wall will be exposed, it needs a top cap. Top off a single-wythe wall with a row of stretchers. Cap a double-wythe wall with a row of headers, or make a rowlock cap—this consists of a row of headers on their sides. You also can cap walls with cast concrete or limestone.

MORTAR JOINTS: At right are eight common joints. Most are easy to make. Select a jointing tool with a shape to match the joint.

Concave and *V joints* effectively keep water from entering the joint. This is especially important in cold climates, where water can freeze and expand, damaging the mortar.

Flush joints are quick and easy to make—just scrape the mortar away. But this technique doesn't compress the mortar well and can leave gaps.

Weathered joints resist weathering but are structurally weak. Make them with the tip of a trowel held at an angle.

Several joints do a poor job of shedding water and so shouldn't be used outdoors or anywhere they'll be subject to freezing water. Among them are *extruded* joints. These are the easiest to make—simply let the mortar mush out and leave it. It has a pleasant rustic look. A *struck* joint is both weak and liable to let water in. A *raked* joint produces dramatic shadow lines. A *beaded* joint is the most difficult to make and is easily damaged by weather.

Concave (good)

V joint (good)

Flush (fair)

Weathered (fair)

Extruded (poor)

Struck (poor)

Raked (poor)

Beaded (poor)

Running bond, limestone cap

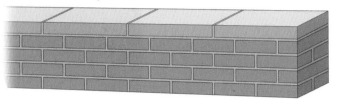

Flemish bond, header cap

CAPS FOR BRICK WALLS

English bond, rowlock cap

SUPPORTING VENEER AND FREESTANDING WALLS

A brick wall—whether veneer or freestanding—must rest on a supporting base that will not move. If the base moves, the mortar will crack.

Brick veneer over a frame building provides no structural strength, only good looks and some insulation. Support the wall with either a concrete beam or an angle-iron ledge.

To build a concrete beam, dig a trench about 1 foot deep and 18 inches wide around the foundation of the structure. Drill holes in the foundation every 2 feet. Insert rebar in the holes so it protrudes 8 inches or so into the trench, then fill the trench with concrete.

To install an angle-iron ledge, buy a piece of 4×4 angle iron called "metal shelf," cut to length. Attach it firmly to the foundation with lag screws and masonry anchors every foot or so.

Build short freestanding masonry walls on a footing that's twice as wide as the width of the wall and as deep as its width. In climates subject to frost heave, dig below the frost line and allow for both the thickness of the concrete and a 4-inch bed of gravel for drainage (see page 26–27).

PREPARING FOR VENEER

Remove the siding, and staple a layer of house wrap or builder's felt to the sheathing underneath to provide a moisture barrier. Remove window and door moldings. Be aware that after adding veneer, moldings and windowsills will no longer fit. You'll need to either replace the original molding with thicker

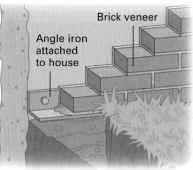

Brick veneer
Angle iron attached to house

To keep mortar from cracking, the support for a veneer wall must be attached to the house's foundation so that it settles as the house settles.

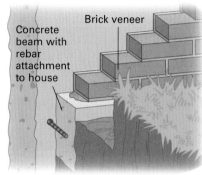

Brick veneer
Concrete beam with rebar attachment to house

pieces or add filler pieces to extend the original moldings and windowsills farther out from the wall.

Use a story pole or mason's rule to determine the height at which the wall should begin so that you can position a course of rowlocks or headers just below door and window openings (see page 66).

For a short planter like this, install a concrete footing, after laying it out with a framing square and chalk line. Use spacers to lay the first course in a dry run.

Concrete footing

DRAINAGE FOR A RETAINING WALL

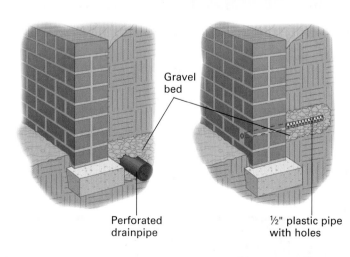

Gravel bed

Perforated drainpipe

½" plastic pipe with holes

Without adequate drainage, water pressure can build up behind a retaining wall and crack it. To remedy, dig a trench at least 8 inches deep and wide behind the foundation (*far left*). Shovel gravel into it, making one end higher than the other. Lay perforated drainpipe, holes facing down, on the gravel. The slope of the gravel directs water away from the wall.

Another solution is to place ½-inch perforated plastic pipe every 4 feet along the wall in the first above-grade course (*left*). Cut an inch off adjacent bricks to fit the pipe. Build up mortar under the pipe at the back of the wall so the pipe tilts up into the backfill. Surround the pipe with a few inches of gravel as you backfill.

LAYING BRICK IN MORTAR

Bricklaying requires concentration and repetitive motions. The more consistent and smooth your motions, the greater the chances you'll build a straight wall.

To ease the job, think it through and set up the work site with care. Arrange all materials so they are within easy reach, remove any obstacles to and in the work site, and avoid working in awkward positions. When digging the footing, don't throw the dirt where it will be in the way of deliveries. And have the truck driver unload brick and other materials where you'll use them. When building a wall taller than 5 feet, use strong and secure scaffolding so you don't have to worry about your footing.

Well-mixed mortar is just dry enough to cut without losing its shape. A trowelful like this is about enough to bed three bricks.

MIXING AND TESTING MORTAR

Watch a bricklaying crew for a while and see what happens when a laborer mixes mortar that is too dry or too wet. You'll quickly learn how important bricklayers think mortar mix is. They are not being unreasonable. If mortar is the wrong consistency, laying a wall is difficult.

Select the correct mortar strength for the project (*see page 61*), and either buy dry-mix bags or arrange for bulk delivery of sand, lime, and portland cement.

Mix a small amount of mortar—enough for an hour's work or so—in a wheelbarrow or a trough. To save your back, place the trough where you won't have to bend low to reach it.

First blend the dry ingredients thoroughly. Then add water, but not too much at once. It is much easier to add more water than to add more dry ingredients. Stir the mortar with a mason's hoe. (Concrete is too heavy to mix with a trowel.)

To test the mortar, form it into a series of ridges with a trowel. If the ridges are dry and crumbly, add water. If the ridges slump and don't hold their shape, the mortar is too wet. Add more dry mix. Another test: Pick some mortar up with your trowel and turn it upside down; it should remain stuck to the trowel.

WET OR DRY BRICKS?

Some bricks are so porous that they absorb water from the mortar, which weakens the joint. Other bricks don't. Test your bricks before laying them.

Select a brick, and pencil a circle about the size of a quarter on its face. Pour ½ teaspoon of water onto the circle, then time how quickly the water soaks into the brick. If the brick absorbs the water in 90 seconds or less, wet the bricks before laying them.

Here's an easy way to do that. Spread out several dozen at a time and spray them on all sides with a hose. Let the surfaces dry before using them—you want the moisture in the brick, not on its face. Wet surfaces will not bond with mortar.

THROWING MORTAR

If you have never worked with bricks and mortar before, practice first and be patient. Handling a brick, mortar, and a trowel at the same time will seem awkward at first; but bricklaying is very repetitive, and you will eventually develop a level of comfort.

Don't *place* the mortar with a trowel. Throw it—like you would fling water out of a glass (it's all in the wrist). To practice this technique, place a shovelful of mortar on a

Don't place mortar slowly and carefully; crooked lines will result. Instead, practice until you can throw the mortar fairly quickly, using a smooth slinging motion. Slice off excess mortar with quick motions as well.

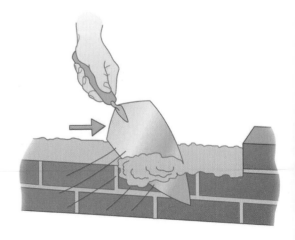

mortarboard. With a brick trowel, cut off a section of the mortar at the edge. Shape it with the trowel so it's roughly the length and width of the trowel, then slide the edge of the trowel under the mortar in one quick motion. Once the trowel is under the mortar, pick it up. Then, flick your wrist in a snapping motion so that the mortar moves slightly up and down back onto the trowel; this bonds the mortar to the trowel. You will have enough mortar on the trowel to bed about three bricks.

Now comes the part that takes practice, where you throw the mortar rather than place it. Tilt the trowel, and sling the mortar from the trowel onto the brick bed, pulling the trowel back toward yourself as you sling (fling the water and pull back). The mortar should slide off the edge of the trowel and land firmly, which helps it adhere to the bed. Start by trying to cover two brick lengths with one throw; when you have mastered that, move on to three or four brick lengths.

Spread the mortar to an even thickness of about 1 inch, then use the trowel to trim the excess along the edges of the brick. Add that mortar to the bed, or put it back on the mortarboard.

THREE BASIC STEPS OF BRICK LAYING

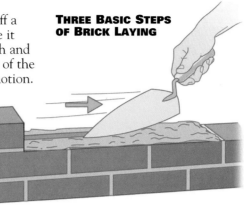

1. Make a light furrow in the bed of mortar.

2. "Butter" the end of the brick.

3. Push the brick into place.

LAYING BRICKS

Once the mortar is spread, lightly furrow the center of the mortar bed with the tip of the trowel. This makes it easier to lay the bricks level. Avoid making a deep furrow, which can leave an air gap under the brick. Set the corner brick in place, tap it gently, and check it for level.

After laying the first brick, "butter" the end of the next brick. Hold it in one hand with the end tipped at a 45-degree angle. Place a small amount of mortar on the trowel, slapping it on the end of the brick with a sharp downward scraping motion.

You don't simply set a brick in place; you shove it. So, after buttering the end, place the brick on the mortar bed and push it firmly against the brick already in place. When you shove the brick correctly, mortar will squish out the sides and top of the joint. Skim off that excess with the trowel, and butter the end of the next brick with it. Rap the placed bricks with the end of the trowel handle to set and level them.

If you set a brick too low, lift it out, add new mortar, and lay it again. Don't simply pull it up a bit; that would leave a gap where water could enter and cause damage.

For a short wall, lay successive courses, and check frequently for level.

MORTAR MANAGEMENT

Mixing mortar to the correct consistency is only the first step. Depending on air temperature and humidity, mortar can begin drying out in as little as 15 minutes. Or it may remain unchanged for an hour.

Keep mortar in the shade whenever possible. If it starts to dry out, add a very small amount of water and remix it. But if it starts to harden, throw it out.

If the temperature is below 40°F, wait for a warmer day to work with mortar. Low temperatures can weaken it.

BUILDING A BRICK WALL

Build a garden wall with two interlocking courses. Every fourth course, embed corrugated metal brick ties at 3-foot intervals. Cap it with flat-laid bricks, formed concrete, or limestone header.

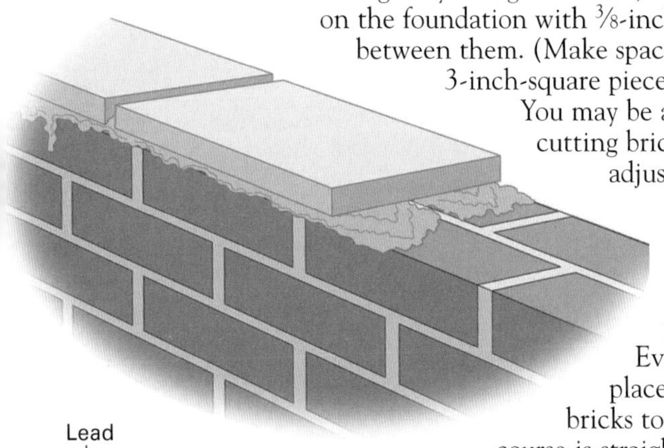

As a bricklayer, you have to be a bit of a juggler with several balls in the air at once. At the same time you are concentrating on correctly laying the bricks in mortar, you must make sure that the courses are level, straight, and plumb. None of these tasks is difficult, but it takes practice before you can do them all at the same time. Like the juggler, once you've mastered the technique, it won't seem difficult at all.

SHORT PLANTER OR WALL

For a small project, such as a planter or a garden wall less than 3 feet high and 8 feet long, simply install a footing (*see pages 26–27*) and lay the bricks in successive courses.

Begin by doing a test run, setting the bricks on the foundation with ⅜-inch spacers between them. (Make spacers by cutting 3-inch-square pieces of plywood.) You may be able to avoid cutting bricks by slightly adjusting spacing. Lay the first course using the techniques shown on pages 64–65. Every so often, place a level on the bricks to check that the course is straight and level. If not, tap the bricks down, or remove the mortar and start again.

Begin the next course with a half brick (or a header on a double-wythe wall) to offset the joints. Add courses until the wall is the desired height. Strike the joints as you go, before the mortar hardens (*see page 67*).

BUILDING A WALL WITH LEADS

For walls taller than a couple of feet, first build up the corners, then fill in the space between. These corners are called *leads*. Laying leads saves time in the long run and helps you keep the courses straight because you can stretch a mason's line the length of the wall and follow that line, rather than checking continually with a level.

Build a simple lead at the end of a wall, and a corner lead—running in two directions—for a wall's corner. When you lay out a corner lead, keep in mind that the number of bricks in the bottom course of the lead (adding together those on both sides of the corner) equals the number of courses high that the finished corner will be. So if your wall will be nine courses high, lay out five bricks along one leg of the corner and four along the other. (*See the illustration below.*)

The lead forms stair steps, half a brick at a time. To make sure all the bricks are properly aligned, lay a level or straightedge from top to bottom at a 45-degree angle against the "steps." The corners of all the bricks should just touch the straightedge. If a brick is out of line, tap it gently into place, but don't move a top or bottom brick.

Once you've built the leads, stretch a taut mason's line from lead to lead for each course. Work toward the center, buttering and setting bricks in mortar and seeing that they nearly touch the line. The last brick in a course is called the closure brick. Butter it on both ends and shoehorn it into place.

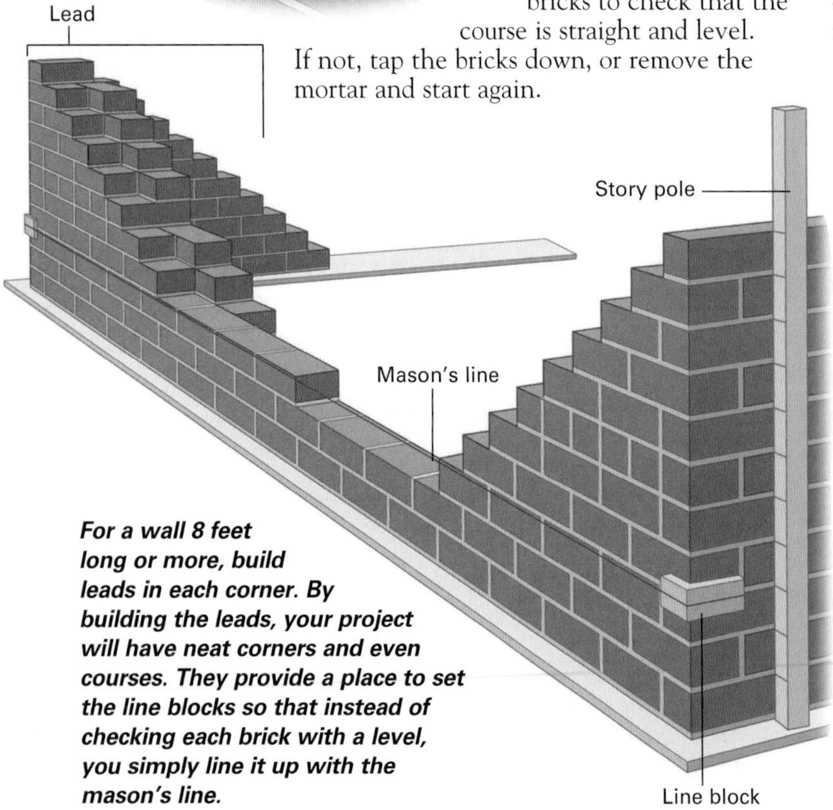

BUILDING A VENEER WALL

After preparing the house for veneer (*see page 63*), test-lay a course of bricks. It may turn out that the bricks plus their mortar joints fall short of the actual dimensions. To avoid cutting many small pieces, you can make the joints slightly thinner or thicker. Space the bricks evenly, then mark their positions with lines on the foundation.

Remove the test course, throw a bed of mortar, then lay the brick, leaving a ½-inch gap between the brick and the house wall. Every four or five bricks, check for level and plumb and that brick faces line up.

Lead

Story pole

Mason's line

For a wall 8 feet long or more, build leads in each corner. By building the leads, your project will have neat corners and even courses. They provide a place to set the line blocks so that instead of checking each brick with a level, you simply line it up with the mason's line.

Line block

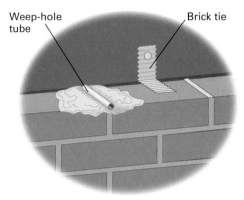

Weep-hole tube Brick tie

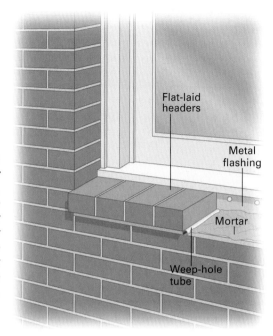

Left: Tie veneer to the house wall with brick ties, and set weep-hole tubes to let moisture escape.

Right: When capping a veneer wall at a sill, slope the cap bricks to allow drainage away from the window. Caulk between the bricks and sill.

Flat-laid headers

Metal flashing

Mortar

Weep-hole tube

On the first above-grade course, set weep-hole tubes in the mortar every 2 feet for drainage. Every 16 vertical inches, install brick ties about 3 feet apart. (Both weep-hole tubes and brick ties are available from your masonry supplier.) Nail the ties into a wall stud and embed them in mortar. Build leads and use lines and line blocks as you would for a standard wall. Where a window interrupts the wall, string a line across it to ensure the courses on both sides line up.

When the rows reach the bottom of a windowsill, spread mortar on the top course under the window, then install metal flashing by nailing it to the house and embedding it in the mortar. Throw mortar on the flashing, then lay rowlock (bricks on edge) or flat-laid headers on it. The sill bricks should extend past the face of the wall an inch or so. Mound up extra mortar near the house so you can slope the sill bricks away from the house. Also, install weep-hole tubes every foot or so.

At the top of a window or door, install angle iron so it extends at least 6 inches on each side of the frame. The mortar on the angle iron will be very thin to match the rest of the joint line.

TOOLING THE JOINTS

Keep a careful watch on the mortar as you work, and tool—or finish—the joints at the right time—when the mortar will just accept a thumbprint with firm pressure. Jointing not only gives you the look you want, but also fills in gaps in the mortar and keeps out moisture.

Use a jointing tool that gives you the joint of your choice (see page 62). Press the tool into the joint and slide it back and forth until the joint is smooth. Tool the vertical (head) joints first, then the horizontal (bed) joints. If the joint doesn't have enough mortar in it, place a small amount of mortar on a trowel. Hold the trowel at right angles to the wall and against the joint. Push the mortar off the trowel with the jointer, just as you would do if you were tuckpointing (see pages 80–81).

As soon as you tool the joints, sweep away loose particles of mortar with a soft brush. If mortar sticks to the bricks, immediately clean it off with a wet sponge.

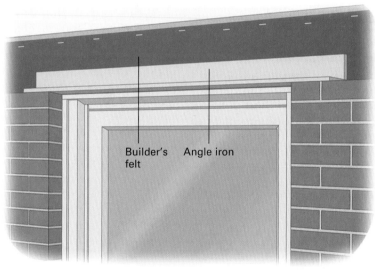

Builder's felt Angle iron

Use a 3½-inch by 3½-inch angle iron to span the gap above doors and windows.

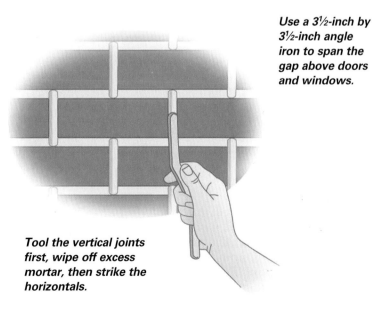

Tool the vertical joints first, wipe off excess mortar, then strike the horizontals.

BUILDING A BLOCK WALL

Concrete block is much larger than brick, which means that projects go together faster. But the work is more physically demanding because the blocks are mighty heavy. Have them delivered and placed in a convenient spot, and make sure you have plenty of help.

PREPARATION

Plan the job carefully to minimize cutting. If possible, build the footing so that its length is divisible by 16 inches (the length of a standard block plus a mortar joint). Use a running bond pattern, which is both easy and strong.

The footing (*see pages 26–27*) should be twice as wide as the block and at least 8 inches thick. Even if it is not required by local building codes, install reinforcement. Embed 32-inch lengths of vertical rebar (bent at their ends) in the concrete when you pour the footing. Set them on 32-inch centers so that the bent ends poke through the cells of the block.

Do not wet the blocks. If it looks like rain or heavy dew, cover them.

To solve any problems before applying mortar, lay the first course in a dry run, spaced with ⅜-inch plywood to represent the mortar joint. Snap a chalk line on the footing exactly 1½ inches outside the block line. Use this chalk line as a guide for the first course; it will be far enough away not to be covered by mortar spread on the footing.

A block wall calls for many of the techniques that apply to a brick wall. Chalk a layout line, then lay the first course in a 1-inch-thick mortar bed. Build leads and string mason's line to maintain even courses.

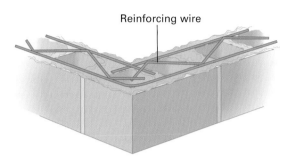

Place reinforcing wire on every other course. Embedded in the mortar, it adds a great deal of strength to a block wall.

LAYING THE BLOCKS

Concrete block has a top and bottom. Look at the thickness of its sides around the webs: They're wider on top. Always place the wider edges up so that the block holds mortar well. You will quickly get the hang of this because block is easier to pick up by the wider edges. Spread mortar only on the outside edges of the block, not on the cross web.

STARTING WITH LEADS: Build leads by spreading a solid 1-inch-thick three-block-long layer of mortar on the footing. The mortar should be about an inch wider than the block on each side and ½ inch from the chalk line. Position a block and press it down until the mortar is compressed to ⅜ inch thick. Use a piece of 2×4 to see that the blocks are 1½ inches from the layout line. Check for level and plumb.

Butter one end of the next block, and press it into place against the first one. Level and plumb each block as you go. On ends without corners, every other course after the first course should start and end with a half block. In a well-constructed corner lead, you should be able to lay a straightedge on the "steps" between the top and bottom blocks and it should just touch each block in between.

Every other course, lay reinforcing wire made for your size of concrete block.

FINISHING THE COURSES: For subsequent courses, lay the mortar ¾ inch thick. Stand two or three blocks on end and butter them all at the same time. Tap each block level using the end of the trowel handle, then scrape away squeezed-out mortar. It's better to let mortar drips on the block harden before scraping them off; trying to remove soft mortar can produce smears that are difficult to clean.

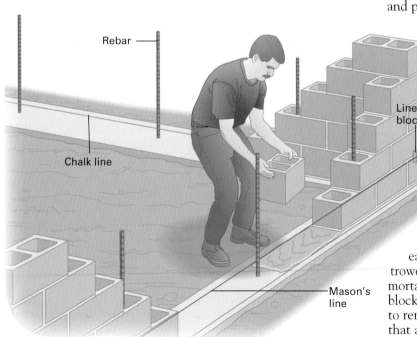

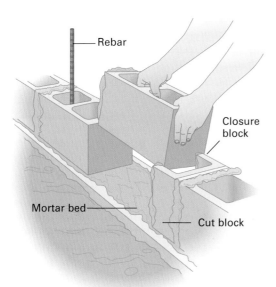

Butter both ends of the closure block and slip it in carefully. Make sure the mortar doesn't scrape off at the ends as you place the block.

To keep each course level and straight, stretch mason's line even with the top of the course to be laid. Each block should be even with the top of the line and about $\frac{1}{16}$ inch (about the thickness of the line) inside it. Don't let the blocks touch the line. If any block needs adjusting, do it while the mortar is still wet.

The last block, or closure block, is the trickiest one. Butter both of its ends and both adjoining blocks. Hold the closure block directly above the opening, then push it down with one smooth motion. Immediately scrape off excess mortar, then tap the block until it is level and straight. If the mortar falls off the block on your first attempt, pull out the block, remortar everything, and try again.

CONTROL JOINTS: These vertical breaks in a wall allow its sections to move up and down but maintain lateral rigidity when temperatures change. You need control joints

SURFACE-BONDED BLOCK

Here's an alternate method for laying concrete block—one that will save you work. Mortar only the first course of blocks to anchor them to the footing. Stack the rest of the blocks on top of each other without mortar. Then cover the wall with a special surface-bonding agent made of portland cement and fiberglass. This method produces a strong wall, but check to see whether it conforms to your local building codes.

REINFORCING A BLOCK WALL

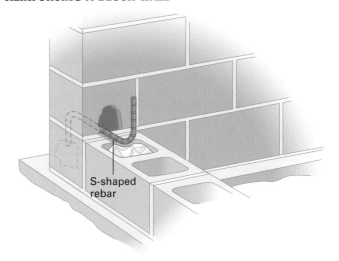

To tie into another block wall, break a hole with a chisel and hammer. Wad newspaper in the opening so you don't have to fill it entirely. With a chisel, cut a channel in the new block, and lay an S-shaped piece of rebar as shown. Fill the cavity with mortar.

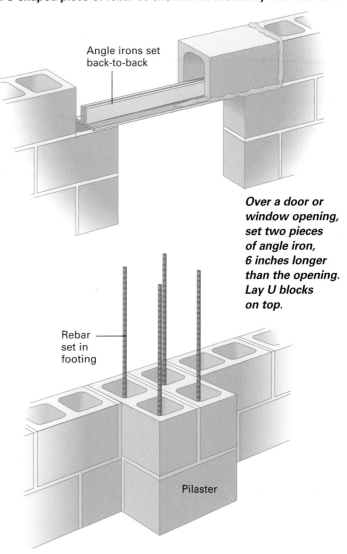

Over a door or window opening, set two pieces of angle iron, 6 inches longer than the opening. Lay U blocks on top.

To strengthen a long wall, you may have to build a column called a pilaster. The footing must extend under the pilaster to support it. Embed 6-foot-long rebar in the footing. As you set the blocks, offset the joints. Fill the cells with concrete to the top of the pilaster.

BUILDING A BLOCK WALL
continued

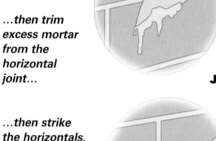

Use a convex jointer on verticals first...

...then trim excess mortar from the horizontal joint...

...then strike the horizontals.

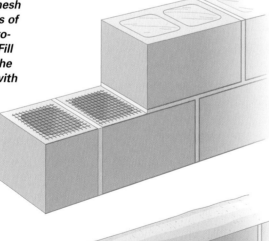

in any block wall that's 60 feet or longer. Installing them every 20 feet will minimize the chance that the wall will crack.

One type of control joint, made of rubber in the shape of a cross, fits into the grooved ends of block made for this purpose. Another type has tongue-and-groove ends; one locks into the other. Check with your building department to see which type they recommend. After the wall is finished, fill control joints with concrete caulk.

FINISHING THE JOINTS: As you work, continually scrape excess mortar from the joints. Reuse it by mixing it with the mortar on the board.

Once the mortar in the joints has hardened so it just barely accepts a thumbprint with firm pressure, tool it. First, use a convex jointer to compress all the joints. Trim off the excess with the edge of the trowel. Let the mortar set up a little more, then retool the joints—the vertical ones first, then the horizontal ones—to form a pleasing, distinct joint (*see page 67*).

When the mortar has dried, brush the wall with a wire or other stiff brush to remove any dirt and small fragments of mortar.

CAPPING A WALL: A cap not only gives the wall a finished appearance, it also keeps out moisture. To cap the wall with flagstone or flat concrete block, fill the cells of the top course with pieces of scrap block and concrete, then with mortar. The cap should overhang the wall about ¾ inch so that water drips off rather than entering the wall.

To cap off with mortar, cover the cells of the second-to-last course with wire mesh or roofing felt. Then fill the top course cells with mortar or concrete mix. While this is still fresh, begin laying on the top layer of the concrete cap, building it up in the center so it sheds water. Finish by rounding this layer over the top of the wall with a trowel, much like you would smooth frosting on a cake. Use a brush to remove any ridges in the mortar.

To cap blocks off with mortar, place wire mesh over the cells of the second-to-last course. Fill the cells of the top course with mortar.

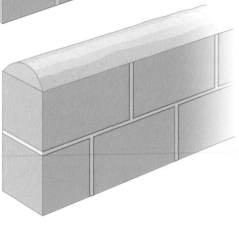

Continue adding mortar to produce a rounded top so that water can drain off easily. Smooth with a trowel, then with a brush.

STUCCOING A BLOCK WALL

Concrete block has an industrial appearance, but that can be remedied by stuccoing over it. First coat the blocks with a latex bonding agent. Then apply the stuccos as described on pages 78–79.

BUILDING AN INTERLOCKING-BLOCK RETAINING WALL

Many manufacturers make concrete block specifically to hold back earth, and each product has a different system of interlocking. A wall built from interlocking block is one of the simplest masonry projects possible. It needs neither mortar nor a footing. It does require a footing trench, and that calls for plenty of digging and hauling. Retaining walls up to 3 feet high usually don't require inspection, but for a higher wall, check your local codes.

LAY OUT: Stake out and string the area for the base of the wall. Then excavate a trench about 1 foot deep and 16 inches wider than the block. Place landscaping fabric on the slope but not in the bottom of the trench. Fill the trench with gravel, compacting it to 6 inches deep.

ALLOW FOR DRAINAGE: Water trapped behind a retaining wall often leads to wall failure, so provide a way for it to escape. If water is a minor problem, it will simply seep through the face of the blocks and down through the gravel. For areas that receive heavy rain, embed perforated drainpipe, with the holes facing down, in the gravel behind the first course. The drainpipe should lie at a slope so it can carry water toward an area you don't mind getting wet, or into a dry well (see page 47).

FIRST COURSE: Lay the first course of block in the trench—it will be below grade—or as recommended by the manufacturer. Align and level each block. If the blocks have cells, fill them with gravel. Drive lengths of rebar or fiberglass anchoring pins through the blocks and into the ground.

ABOVE GROUND: Lay the first course of above-grade block, and backfill with gravel. Set another two courses and backfill again with more gravel. At the second-to-last course, pull the landscaping fabric over the gravel, then backfill the space between the retaining wall and the slope with soil. Tamp it down thoroughly.

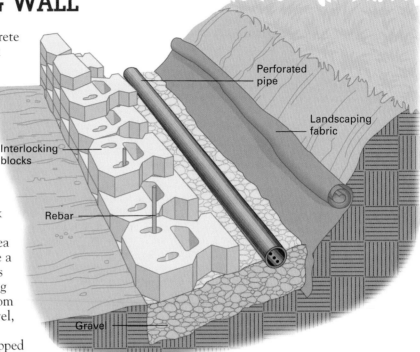

Interlocking blocks

Rebar

Perforated pipe

Landscaping fabric

Gravel

Pieces of rebar or fiberglass anchoring pins help hold the blocks in place; gravel and perforated pipe prevent damage from water pressure.

Interlocking blocks

Interlocking blocks are ideal for building raised planting beds three or four courses tall.

WORKING WITH STONE

Stone has a pleasing, random appearance once it's installed. A few tips and techniques will take some of the strain out of getting it in place. Plan carefully and use labor-saving tools whenever possible.

GATHERING AND HAULING STONE

To harvest stone from a field or riverbed, you'll need a long pry bar, a crowbar, and an understanding of leverage. Remember—when you lift, use your legs, not your back.

To move stones that are small but too heavy to carry, use a garden cart or a child's metal wagon. Tip it on end so that you can push or roll the stones into it.

A hand truck also works, but its small wheels may bog down in soft soil. Bring along boards on which to roll it. When moving stone in a wheelbarrow over soft ground, put the load toward the back to keep the weight off the front wheel.

If you plan to move large amounts of stone, buy or build a stone boat, basically a sturdy sled with wide iron or steel runners. Because the stone boat is low to the ground, all you have to do is push or roll the stones onto it. And you can chain it to a trailer hitch and drag it across a field.

Assemble all the stones in one place before loading them on a trailer to transport them to the building site. Use a low trailer so you won't have to lift the stones too high. Roll the stones up a long, sturdy ramp, either on log rollers or by flipping them end-over-end. Balance the load so as to place only a moderate amount of weight on the truck.

Another option is to rent a small earth-moving machine with a scoop loader. With it, you can easily pick up large stones and load them onto a truck.

ESTIMATING STONE

If you are building a rubble wall from collected fieldstone, it is difficult to know when you have accumulated enough. Try to have more on hand than you think you will need, because many of the stones you select won't fit into the wall.

When buying stone, first calculate the cubic footage (length times width times height, in feet) of the wall. (For patios or walks, figure the area, in square feet: length times width.) With those dimensions, the stone yard staff can estimate how much material you will need. They'll probably add 10 percent to the total (25 percent if buying rubble) to allow for breakage and stones that won't fit. Stone yards often sell stone by the cubic yard; 1 cubic yard is 27 cubic feet.

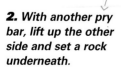

Stone boat

Hand truck

A stone boat allows you to slide heavy stones across terrain where wheels would get stuck. A hand truck is the easiest way to move heavy objects on solid ground. When loading the trailer or at the job site, roll stones up a ramp so you don't have to lift the entire stone.

Roll stone up a ramp end-over-end.

MOVING STONE

1. Dig a hole around the stone. Using a 2×4 or 4×4 wooden block as a fulcrum under the pry bar, raise the stone and place a small rock underneath it.

2. With another pry bar, lift up the other side and set a rock underneath.

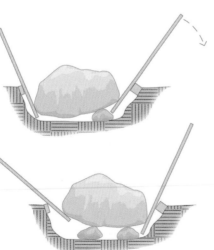

3. Pry from both sides and work a board under the stone as a plank.

4. Work the stone up the plank.

TOOLS

You can shape stone by chipping, cutting, or splitting. It takes a while to get the hang of these skills, so practice for a few hours on waste rock.

Stoneworking tools are not expensive. Buy most of the ones listed here if you plan to do much stonework. One or two of these tools may surprise you with their usefulness in other projects.

A heavy *stonemason's hammer* (5 to 8 pounds) provides the necessary striking weight. A carpenter's hammer is too light and may chip. Use a *striking hammer* for driving wedges and chisels, and a *mason's hammer* to chip off corners.

Have several stonemason's chisels on hand. A *pitching chisel* cuts a narrow path through rock. A *bull-point* or *pointing chisel* is good for chipping away small areas. Use a *stone chisel,* which resembles a brickset but is heavier, for most stone cutting. With a *toothed chisel* you can cut a surface with decorative ridges. (Names for chisels vary from region to region.)

For splitting stone, buy a number of *feathers* and *wedges,* also called featherwedges or splitting wedges. Typically, these consist of two short wedge-shaped metal rods (feathers) that you insert into a hole and force apart with another rod (the wedge) driven between them. Featherwedges are difficult to find but are worth the search. Try a local rental center or a masonry supply yard.

Protective eyewear is essential when cutting stone. Wear shatterproof *safety goggles* that fit firmly at the sides of your eyes, or safety glasses with corner shields. Wear a pair of leather work gloves whenever you cut and lift stone.

Other basic masonry tools, such as a *shovel, wheelbarrow,* and *brick* and *pointing trowels* can save labor. Also plan to have on hand a *power drill* with *masonry bits* and a *circular saw* with a *masonry blade.*

CUTTING FIELDSTONE: Place the stone to be cut on a surface that is firm but resilient, such as the ground, a bed of sand, or scrap pieces of wood. Don't place it on concrete or other stones; the stone may crack in the wrong place.

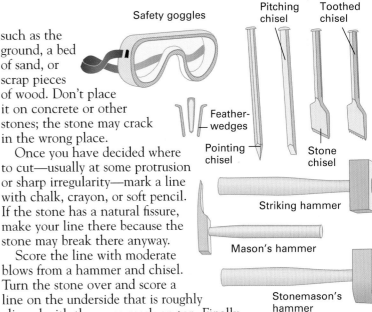

Safety goggles | Pitching chisel | Toothed chisel | Featherwedges | Pointing chisel | Stone chisel | Striking hammer | Mason's hammer | Stonemason's hammer

Once you have decided where to cut—usually at some protrusion or sharp irregularity—mark a line with chalk, crayon, or soft pencil. If the stone has a natural fissure, make your line there because the stone may break there anyway.

Score the line with moderate blows from a hammer and chisel. Turn the stone over and score a line on the underside that is roughly aligned with the score mark on top. Finally, place the chisel on the mark and strike it very sharply with the hammer. Not all stone will crack; set aside the ones that won't, and try others.

After the cut is complete, dress the edge (remove sharp irregularities) with a pointing chisel. Place the point of the chisel at the base of the bump, and rap it sharply with the hammer.

SPLITTING LARGE STONES: You can split large flat stones, 3 or 4 feet across, with several pairs of feathers and wedges. (You also use featherwedges to split concrete.)

First, chalk a cutting line. Then, using a power drill with a masonry bit the diameter of the featherwedge assembly, drill a hole every 8 inches along the line.

Insert the featherwedges into each hole. Gently tap each featherwedge, starting in the middle, then working alternate sides. The pressure should split the rock along the line. If it doesn't, redrill holes at 4-inch intervals and try again.

Take care to not jam the wedges into the feathers so tightly that you can't pull them out. If they do get stuck, pry them out with a crowbar. Place a wood block under the crowbar so it doesn't mar the stone.

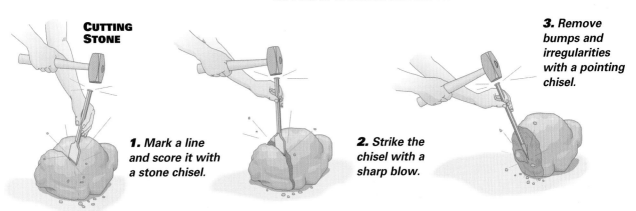

CUTTING STONE

1. Mark a line and score it with a stone chisel.

2. Strike the chisel with a sharp blow.

3. Remove bumps and irregularities with a pointing chisel.

MORTARED STONE WALL

A stone wall built with mortar can work wonders in your landscape. Though it calls for a major investment of time and muscle, once built it will be a long-lasting showpiece in your yard or garden.

PREPARING THE SITE

In general, a stone wall should be about 2 feet thick for every 3 feet of height (for example, 4 feet thick for a 6-foot-high wall). For every 6 inches of additional height, add 4 inches to the width of the base. Actual dimensions may be dictated by local building codes.

A mortared wall is inflexible. Support it on a solid footing; otherwise, it will crack from soil settling or frost heave. (Dry walls can be laid on a bed of gravel; see page 76.)

See pages 26–27 for instructions for laying out and building a wall footing. The footing should be 6 inches wider than the base of the wall and at least 8 inches deep. In areas with cold winters, dig the footing below the frost line. In addition, reinforce the entire trench with two parallel lengths of ½-inch rebar.

If the stone wall will be backed by earth, as in a planting box, install weep holes. The weep holes can be as simple as unmortared gaps in the base. Or use weep-hole tubes (see page 67). See page 63 for solutions to serious drainage problems. You may choose to batter a mortared wall—that is, taper it so the top is narrower than the bottom—but it is not necessary (see page 76 for instructions).

BUILDING THE WALL

The key to building a sturdy, pleasing wall is stone selection. Carefully select and fit each stone before applying mortar. Use stones that nest comfortably against the surrounding stones. Mortar alone will not hold it in place; gravity will eventually prevail. Wedge small stones between large stones to fill any voids.

CLEAN THE STONES: Dirt, moss, and sand on the stones will prevent the mortar from bonding well. Brush them clean, using water if necessary. Allow them to dry; if stones are wet, mortar will ooze out of the joints and will be difficult to clean off.

LAY THE FIRST COURSE: Start with a dry run, arranging the largest stones on the footing and turning them back and forth to get a good fit. The wall will be at least two stones thick, with small rubble and mortar wedged between large stones to fill voids.

Mix the mortar as follows: 1 part portland cement, 1 part lime, and 6 parts sand. Add water slowly, but only enough that the mortar is stiff and does not flow. Remove the first course of stones, and place them on the ground without changing their alignment, so you can put them back the same way. Spread a 2-inch-thick layer of mortar on the footing, and set the stones back in place.

SET THE FIRST COURSE: Place a couple of shovelfuls of mortar on a piece of plywood, and keep it on the ground beside you. Don't be delicate: Throw mortar from the trowel onto the footing.

Jab the mortar with the tip of the trowel to remove any air bubbles, then set the stone in place. Rap the stone firmly with the end of the trowel handle to seat it and to force out any air bubbles. Scrape off the excess mortar and throw the scrapings into the center of the wall.

In many weather conditions, mortar will begin to set in about 30 minutes, so spread only as much as you can use in that amount of time. If the mortar in the wheelbarrow gets too

BUILDING A MORTARED STONE WALL

1. Once the reinforced footing has cured, lay the first stone course, infilling between large stones with rubble.

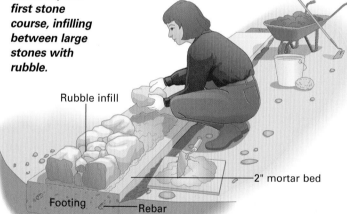

Rubble infill

2" mortar bed

Footing

Rebar

2. As you add courses, have a variety of different sizes and shapes of stones within easy reach so you can easily find the right one for each situation.

Line level

Mason's line

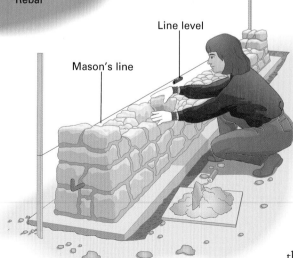

stiff while you are getting started, add a little water. To keep the stones clean as you work, have a bucket of water with a large sponge handy to immediately wipe off any spills.

BUILD THE ENDS: After you have set the first course on the footing, stretch mason's line between two stakes driven at each end of the wall. Set the line 3 to 4 inches above the top of the next course—as a rough guide to keep the wall level and plumb. Interlock the stones as much as possible for strength and stability. Save some flat stones for capping the wall.

LAY THE MIDDLE COURSES: The motto for a good stonemason is, "One rock over two, two rocks over one." Aligning joints directly over each other weakens the wall.

Begin the second course by dry-fitting several stones until you have a smooth and stable fit. Then remove them, throw mortar onto the top of the first course, and fit the stones back into place. When fitting two stones side by side, spread mortar on the one already in place.

Every two or three courses, lay bond stones, which span the thickness of the wall to tie it together. Place these about 4 feet apart horizontally and approximately halfway up the wall, or more often if you have enough stones of the right size.

Build only one or two courses of the wall per day. The weight of additional courses forces mortar out of uncured joints.

JOINTING: You can leave the mortar in the joints so it is flush with the wall face, or rake the joints out. Raked joints add definition to the wall.

Because the stones are so thick and broad, you can remove up to ½ inch of mortar in the joints without weakening the wall. This is most easily done with the end of an old broom handle or a piece of ¾-inch pipe. Mortar is ready to be raked when pressing it firmly leaves only a shallow thumbprint—usually, about half an hour after applying the mortar. If you are building a long wall, be sure to joint the first part before the mortar sets.

Rake the joints to the depth you prefer. Then with a soft brush, such as an old paintbrush, remove the excess mortar. For a smoother joint, go over them again with a jointing tool.

CAPPING: An excellent way to finish a wall is to mortar a row of flat bond stones across the top from front to back. Or use contrasting cut stone, such as granite or slate. Set the flat cap stones flush with the stones beneath them with no overhang.

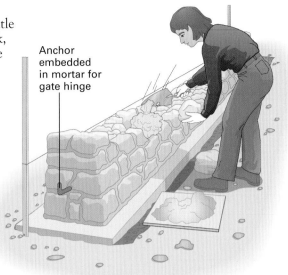

Anchor embedded in mortar for gate hinge

3. Slap the mortar down firmly. After setting a stone in the mortar, immediately wipe away any excess.

4. Place tie stones (or bond stones) on every third or fourth course, positioned every 4 linear feet.

5. The front and back sides of the wall should be battered: As you build the upper courses, the wall should decrease in width about 1 inch per foot of wall height (see page 76). Save some of the flattest and best-looking stones for the cap.

Battered side

DRY STONE WALL

An unmortared wall does not need to rest on a concrete foundation. But it does need a gravel base, and you may have to refit or replace some of the stones every few years; they can become dislodged when water enters the wall and freezes.

PLANNING AND LAYING THE BASE: It is important to batter a dry stone wall—to taper it inward at the top. Make a triangular batter guide from 1×2 or 1×4 lumber. Nail the three pieces together as shown in the illustration below. The side opposite the right-angled base should tilt back 1 inch for every foot of rise.

Lay a dry-set wall so its base is 2 feet thick for every 3 feet of height. If you are building a low retaining wall (2 to 3 feet high) against an existing bank, however, a 1-foot-thick wall will do. In such a case, it is a good idea to batter the dirt bank (taper it into the slope) with a pick and shovel before building the wall. Do not attempt to build a dry stone wall more than 4 feet high; it won't be stable.

Because water can seep through the spaces between dry-laid stones, you won't need weep holes. However, if the site has serious water problems, install drainage like that shown on page 63.

LAYING THE BASE: Excavate a trench about 12 inches deep and fill it with gravel.

You will build the wall by laying two parallel lines of stone and filling in between the stones with small rubble.

BUILDING LEAD ENDS: Build leads at each end of a dry stone wall, much as you do for a brick wall (*see page 66*). Then build the area in between the leads, using a string line as a rough guide for height. Place the stones one on top of two, so they interlock. Also set them with their smoothest edge facing out for a finished appearance. Save some of your flattest stones for capping the wall. If you can't find stones that fit together well, cut them to fit. Take your time, because a tight fit is important to the stability of the entire wall.

LAYING THE MIDDLE COURSES: Lay the remaining courses as described for a mortared stone wall (*see page 75*), using a mason's line to keep the work roughly level. Periodically check the face of the wall with the batter guide; remove and reinstall stones if they are more than 2 inches out of alignment.

Every three or four courses, tie the wall together with bond stones—stones that span the entire thickness of the wall—about every 4 feet horizontally.

CAPPING THE WALL: Lay a series of flat bond stones across the top of the wall, not only to give it a finished appearance but also to hold the wall firmly together. Mortaring this last course in place greatly increases the strength of the wall.

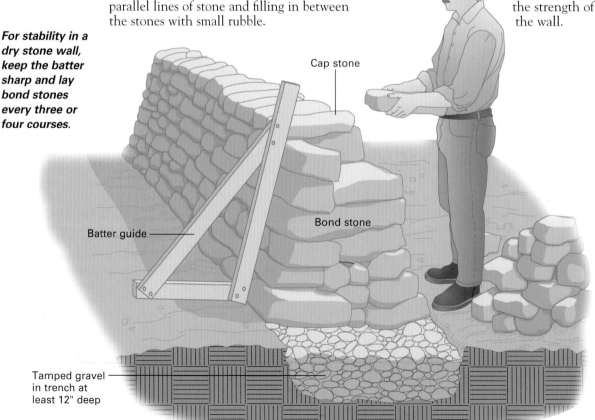

For stability in a dry stone wall, keep the batter sharp and lay bond stones every three or four courses.

Cap stone

Batter guide

Bond stone

Tamped gravel in trench at least 12" deep

GLASS BLOCK

Glass block brings a decorative effect to any wall while providing insulation, security and allowing light to filter in. Special blocks allow ventilation.

PREPARE THE OPENING: First remove the existing window. If the wooden jamb is in good shape, you can install the block inside it. However, by removing all wood and mortaring the block directly to brick or concrete, there's no chance for rot.

For installing against wood, or for interior installations, glass block manufacturers have systems that use clear or white rubber strips and silicone sealer. In such an installation, you need not apply mortar.

MORTARING BLOCKS INDIVIDUALLY: Measure the opening, then purchase enough blocks to fit inside it. Be sure to account for the space between blocks, which should be an inch or less on all sides. Instead of cutting block to fit at the edges, buy two sizes. Also pick up panel anchors, reinforcing wire, and spacers.

Dry-fit some of the blocks to get the hang of how they go together. Use full spacers for four-armed joints, T spacers for three-armed joints, and L spacers at corners. (Make Ts and Ls by snapping off parts of full spacers.)

Install a panel anchor at each bottom corner. Staple foam expansion strips to the side walls to prevent cracking when the house settles. Mix a stiff batch of white glass-block mortar, and lay a bed on the sill. Set spacers in place, then the block. Butter each block on one side where it touches its neighbor, but not an expansion strip. For each succeeding course, spread a bed of mortar on top of the set blocks. Every third course, attach panel anchors on each side of the window frame. When all the blocks are laid, twist off the face tabs on the spacers and fill the holes with mortar. Strike the joints and wipe the blocks clean. After the mortar sets, caulk the sides and the top.

PREASSEMBLED BLOCK: To save work and time, order glass block preassembled to fit the opening. Measure carefully. To be completely sure of the dimensions, remove the existing window, measure, then replace the window. If the opening is out of square, give the dimensions to a supplier specializing in glass block to ensure proper fit.

The supplier will assemble the blocks and hold them together with a metal strap. The assembly will be heavy, so have help on hand when you install it. Lay a bed of mortar on the sill, place spacers every foot or so, then gently slide the assembly in place. Fill the sides and top with mortar or thick caulk.

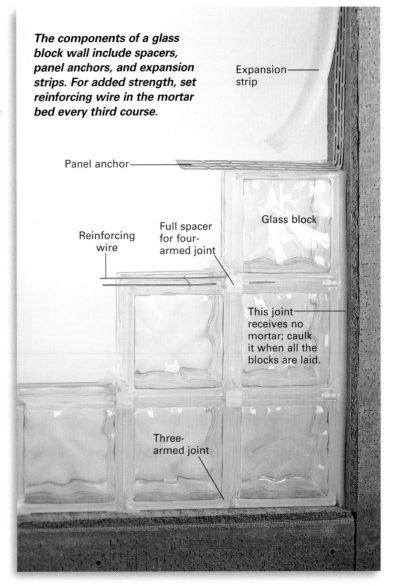

The components of a glass block wall include spacers, panel anchors, and expansion strips. For added strength, set reinforcing wire in the mortar bed every third course.

Expansion strip

Panel anchor

Reinforcing wire

Full spacer for four-armed joint

Glass block

This joint receives no mortar; caulk it when all the blocks are laid.

Three-armed joint

Mortar

Set, don't slide, the glass blocks in place so as not to disturb the mortar bed. Use a jointer to strike the joints. Wipe the glass blocks clean with a soft rag and water. Caulk wherever the blocks join wood or other material.

APPLYING STUCCO

I n some established communities, local masons can tell who stuccoed a wall just by looking at its texture. Stucco reflects the individual personality of the installer, and no two walls are exactly alike.

Stucco is not only an attractive material, it is also very durable. Properly installed, stucco resists cracking for many years. If small cracks appear, timely caulking will prevent serious problems.

Standard stucco is gray, but you can color it by adding oxide pigment to the finish coat. This also keeps you from having to paint. To make white stucco, use white portland cement and white sand.

Whisk broom

Finishing trowel

Stiff masonry brush

PREPARING THE WALL

Remove any siding from the structure, unless its surface is fairly smooth. Staple 15-pound roofing felt (tar paper) over the sheathing, working carefully so there are no wrinkles or bubbles. Then attach wire-mesh lath made for stucco work. This type of lath is "self-furring," meaning that it holds itself slightly off the wall to allow the stucco to adhere firmly. With a helper, roll the mesh out on a flat surface and cut it to fit fairly precisely. Place it carefully, avoid bends and twists, and attach the mesh with 1¼-inch roofing nails spaced no more than 8 inches apart.

To stucco over a block, brick, or concrete wall, first wire-brush or sand away any loose material. (If the wall is painted, the stucco will stick to the paint, which may pull away

Don't be shy about experimenting with stucco textures. The important thing is to be very comfortable with your pattern by the time you start applying it to the wall.

from the masonry.) Fill holes with patching concrete. Finish the preparation by brushing on a latex concrete-bonding agent.

THE FIRST COAT(S)

Mix 1 part portland cement with 3 parts sand and a small amount of lime, which keeps the stucco from setting up too quickly. Apply the first coat, called the scratch coat, using a concrete finishing trowel. Push the mix into the lath, and apply more mix until you have a fairly smooth coat that is ¼ to ½ inch thick. Use long, sweeping strokes to get a uniform thickness.

Once the stucco has begun to stiffen but before it hardens, scratch it with a scarifier. This is a tool that resembles a large comb and gives a "tooth" to the surface so the topcoat will adhere firmly. Scratch to a depth of about ⅛ inch.

Keep the scratch coat moist for two days because it will lose strength if it dries out quickly. Spray it with water every 4 to 6 hours—more often if it is in direct sun or if the air is very dry.

To get a surface that is extremely durable, apply a second base coat soon after the scratch coat hardens. This "brown coat" does not need to be scratched, but keep it moist for two days.

THE FINISH COAT

Now for the artistic part. It is important for your finish coat to look the same over the entire area; achieving that goal may take some practice. Hone your technique by practicing on a

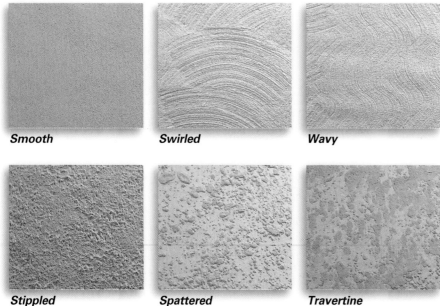

Smooth

Swirled

Wavy

Stippled

Spattered

Travertine

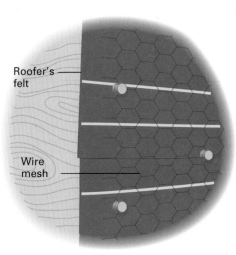

Roofer's felt

Wire mesh

1. Staple roofer's felt, then attach wire mesh with nails.

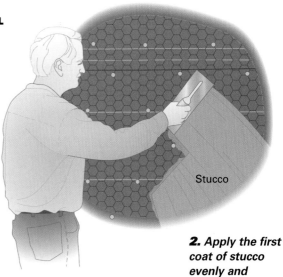

Stucco

2. Apply the first coat of stucco evenly and smoothly.

piece of plywood; have your strokes down pat before working on the wall.

With a concrete finishing trowel, apply the finish coat using long strokes. Keep the leading edge of the trowel only slightly raised for a uniformly smooth finish.

At this point, you have several options. You can leave the wall fairly smooth, with only subtle trowel lines running in several directions. Or you can use a stiff masonry brush to pattern the stucco. Use long, arcing strokes or short, intersecting strokes, or swirl the pattern.

Another way to pattern the stucco is to dip a brush in stucco that is slightly less stiff than the original coat, then spatter the wall. Throw stucco with whiplike motions, overhand, sidearm, and at a 45-degree angle, for an even pattern. Let the spatters dry as they are for a bumpy effect, or wait a few minutes and then very gently smooth them down with a trowel for a raised texture. You can use different-colored stucco for the spattering.

Once the stucco has hardened, caulk the joints at any openings. Wait at least a month before painting the stucco.

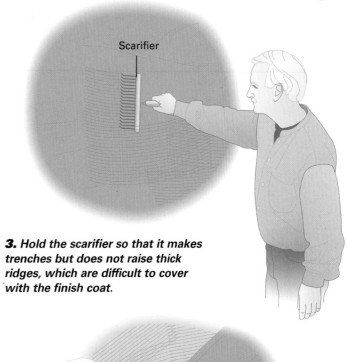

Scarifier

3. Hold the scarifier so that it makes trenches but does not raise thick ridges, which are difficult to cover with the finish coat.

A New Stucco Method

Using aggregated polymer stucco saves time but costs more in materials. To use it, install metal flashing along the bottom of the wall, then cover the wall with roofing felt (tar paper). Next, instead of wire mesh, attach sheets of cement board to the wall with cement-board screws. Cover the cement-board surface with a thin layer of portland cement mixed with water, then trowel on the polymer stucco.

4. Apply the final coat of stucco with a finishing trowel held at a slight angle. The coat should be no more than ¼-inch thick. (See the opposite page for stucco finishing options.)

REPAIRS

As permanent as masonry installations may seem, with time they can crack, chip, or break loose in spalls or pop-outs. In this chapter, you'll find techniques for repairing the most common masonry problems.

Every 20 or 30 years, even the best-laid brick or block wall will show its age. As with people, the joints are the most frail. Mortar may develop cracks, or it may simply wear away until it is unsightly and compromises the wall's strength. The solution is to remove the old mortar and refill the joints with new mortar. This time-consuming job is called tuckpointing or repointing.

Mix 1 part portland cement, 2 parts lime, and 8 parts sand. Add only enough water to make a ball of mortar. Let this mix stand for about 20 minutes, then add just enough more water to make the mixture easy to work. This two-step process rehydrates the mortar, which reduces the tendency of old mortar to draw water out of the new mix and thus weaken it. Even so, spray the wall with water a few minutes before tuckpointing. The color of the new mortar may differ from the old. Try different types of sand as well as coloring agents (let them dry for several days until you find a match).

If the masonry has only a few problem areas, spot-treat them. However, don't simply spread a thin layer of mortar over the old; it will likely crack or flake off. Instead, wearing safety goggles and a dust mask, chisel all cracks and holes so that they are about an inch deep. Mix and apply mortar with a pointing trowel, taking care to work it deeply into the hole. Finish with a pointing tool and brush.

If problems are widespread, tuckpoint the entire wall. Set up scaffolding that is secure and comfortable to avoid having to move a ladder around. Rather than chiseling the cracks—which takes forever—use a 4-inch grinder to remove enough mortar that you can lay in new mortar to a depth of $\frac{1}{2}$ to 1 inch. Start in an area that is not highly visible. Hold the grinder with one elbow pressed against the wall for stability, and lower it slowly into the joint. Hold it firmly so it does not skip away.

After grinding, scrape and brush away loose debris. Load a mortarboard with mortar, and hold it against the wall next to the joint. Push mortar from the mortar board into the joint with a pointing trowel. Fill horizontal joints first, then the verticals. Smooth the new mortar with a jointer, starting with the verticals and finishing with the horizontals.

CRACKS IN BRICK WALLS

Small cracks in an older building can simply be treated by tuckpointing; the building probably will not develop more problems quickly. But cracks in new buildings may be due to settling, and the crack may grow during the next year. To test, place a piece of duct tape tightly over the crack. If it twists, tears, or pulls loose in the next month, the wall is still settling. Wait for settling to end before tuckpointing.

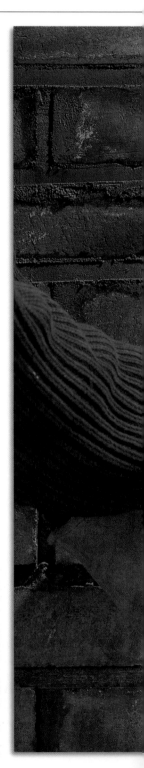

HIGH POINT PUBLIC LIBRARY
HIGH POINT, NORTH CAROLINA

Tuckpointing is necessary when the mortar begins to crack or wear away, compromising the strength of the wall. This fairly exacting repair is within the realm of do-it-yourselfers but is most efficiently done by the pros. Removing old mortar with a power grinder (inset) is the fastest way to get the job done, but in the wrong hands it can permanently damage bricks.

STOPPING LEAKS

Even the best-built basement won't stay dry if water exerts intense pressure against its walls. Whether you find predictable rivulets after every rain, occasional trickles following heavy downpours, or just generally damp conditions, make it a priority to take care of the problem. Moisture not only makes a basement unpleasant, it also weakens your home's foundation over time. The chart on page 83 can help you diagnose and solve the cause of the problem.

KEEPING WATER AWAY

For any moisture problem, first make sure that rainwater and melted snow flow away from the house. Check your gutters and downspouts, watching where the water goes during a rain. If it pours out near the house, install downspout extensions or splash blocks. Long flexible extensions can direct water 8 feet or more away. Also examine the grading around the foundation. If a moat forms around your house after a rain or if water puddles there, build up the soil, sloping it so water flows away.

PATCHING FROM THE INSIDE

Where water seeps slowly or moisture beads up on basement walls, you may be able to solve the problem by applying a cement-based sealer. Wet the wall, mix the sealer's latex and liquid components, then brush the mixture on the wall. Pay special attention to cracks or mortar joints. Keep the sealer moist for a few days so it cures slowly by spraying the wall with water; set a hose nozzle on "mist."

For leaks that occur in single spots on the wall, hydraulic cement will solve the problem permanently. Go outside and place a hose near the foundation about where the leak is.

Set a splash block under a downspout to direct rainwater away from the house's foundation.

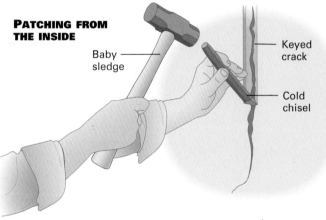

Splash block

PATCHING FROM THE INSIDE

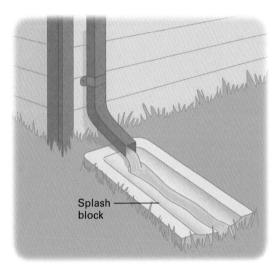

Baby sledge

Keyed crack

Cold chisel

1. To prepare for a hydraulic-cement plug, key a hole that is at least ½ inch deep. Use a cold chisel and a baby sledge. For large jobs, rent an electric chipping hammer.

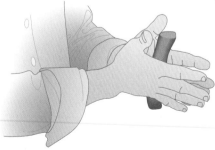

2. Mix and roll the plug until it is smooth and pliable. Use it immediately; it will start to harden very quickly.

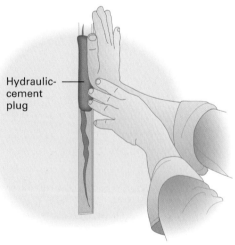

Hydraulic-cement plug

3. Fill the entire hole. You may need to push fairly hard before the leak stops. Keep pushing the original plug; adding a thin layer of extra cement on top of the plug will not help.

BASEMENT PROBLEMS AND SOLUTIONS

Problem/Diagnosis	Solution
Leaks: One or several areas becomes wet during or soon after rainfall. To test, run a hose outside and watch for a trickle of water, usually in the wall but sometimes at the floor. Often such cracks are due to improper concrete pouring or settling of the house.	Add downspout extenders, improve the grading around the foundation, or otherwise keep water from soaking in near the basement wall. Widen and plug cracks or holes with hydraulic cement. If that doesn't solve the leak, either live with the problem or have the wall sealed from the outside *(see below)*.
Seepage: One or several damp areas, usually on a wall near the floor. To test, dry the area and then tape a piece of plastic over it. If water collects behind the plastic, moisture is seeping through the wall.	Improve the grading or use downspout extenders. For minor seepage, brush on a concrete sealer. If seepage is coming up through the floor, repairs will be difficult and costly; install a sump pump to keep the problem manageable.
Condensation: Generally damp walls and pipes that often collect drops of water. Use the same test as for seepage; if water collects on the face of the plastic, it is due to humidity in the air.	Improve ventilation in confined areas by installing an exhaust fan. Install a dehumidifier. Seal walls and pipes to prevent damage from moisture.

Turn on the water, and let it run until water starts coming into the basement. Mark the wet spot or spots, then turn off the hose.

Key the marked area. In other words, chisel the crack so its interior is larger than its face. The key keeps patching material in place. If water flowed out of the bottom of a crack, key the entire crack.

Mix enough hydraulic cement to fill the hole. Stir first with a trowel, then with your hand until the cement is puttylike. Roll the cement into a "snake" between your palms. Turn on the hose and let it run until water flows out of the hole, then press the plug into the hole until the water stops. You may need to press hard. Keep pressure on the plug for several minutes until it hardens and the leak stops. If this plug doesn't work, chisel it out, then chisel the hole more deeply, and plug it again; also try pressing harder on the new plug.

SEALING FROM THE OUTSIDE

If these solutions don't work, your problem is serious. For occasional leaks, install a sump pump, store items off the floor, and simply live with the problem.

For a permanent fix, you will probably want to hire a professional. Some concrete contractors specialize in fixing wet basements. They excavate the area outside the foundation to expose the basement wall and footing. They then install a drainage system, probably a trench of gravel and perforated drainpipe, at the footing. Finally, they coat the wall with a tarlike sealant and perhaps a sheet of plastic. When they're done, backfilled soil should slope away from the house.

Sealant

Plastic sheet

Gravel

Perforated drainpipe

The radical approach to solving basement leaks is to seal a wall from the outside. Drainage at the base must be sloped so it carries water away from the foundation, and the wall must be completely sealed.

PATCHING CONCRETE

Concrete is strong, but it is often subject to enormous pressures. Built-up water pressure, freeze/thaw cycles, and tree roots are the usual culprits when concrete cracks. If a concrete slab is too thin, lacks adequate metal reinforcement, or was laid over a base that is not solid, it will only be a matter of time before it breaks.

CONCRETE MAINTENANCE

A few simple steps can greatly lengthen the life of concrete surfaces. The first step is prevention: Keep moisture damage to a minimum. Painting or staining concrete not only protects surfaces from moisture damage but also improves appearances. To make walks and patios water resistant, apply clear acrylic concrete sealer with a paint roller. To test whether the concrete needs a new coat, sprinkle water on the surface; if it soaks right in, reapply sealer. On aggregate-concrete surfaces, use an aggregate sealer. It prevents freeze/thaw cycles from popping the stones.

The next step is keeping surfaces clean. To remove car oil from driveways and garages, use concrete cleaner and a stiff brush.

Or, soak sawdust in mineral spirits, rub it onto the spot, then sweep.

The last step is making timely repairs. Control joints prevent expansion and contraction from creating large cracks in the concrete. But they can actually cause smaller cracks, which can grow when water puddles in the crack and freezes. Fill small cracks with concrete repair caulk (not with concrete).

REPAIR OR REPOUR?

You can repair most surface problems fairly easily and inexpensively. If cracking results from structural weakness, however, repairs will be a waste of time and money; the only real solution is to tear out the old concrete and start over.

The most common problems are pictured on this page. When diagnosing problems in the concrete surface, check how deep the cracks are. If chunks of concrete are coming loose, don't bother to repair—it's time to repour.

Surface problems like crazing, pop-outs, and spalling do not indicate structural damage. If you leave them alone, however, they can grow worse. Often, applying concrete sealer is all it takes to keep a problem in check.

If the concrete has only a few cracks and its surface is generally solid, concrete caulk or patching compound can add many years

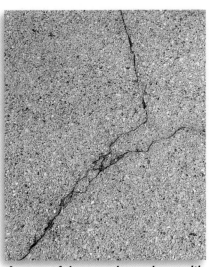

A maze of deep cracks, perhaps with some pieces actually coming loose, indicates that the entire section has failed—most probably because the slab is too thin, is not reinforced, or rests on an unstable base. Don't try to repair it. Break out the whole area, excavate, tamp down a bed of gravel, and pour a new slab.

Small holes, called pop-outs, occur because the surface was not properly floated. Fill larger pop-outs with patching concrete. Pop-outs on a wall should be stable, but those in a patio or a walk in areas subject to freezing may grow.

Improper troweling can result in crazing: a pattern of hairline cracks about ¼ inch deep. Clean it and apply concrete sealer to keep the problem from growing. Or resurface the concrete.

Like crazing, spalling results from improper troweling. The pattern of pits will grow in time. Seal the surface, repour it, or resurface.

If one section is raised above another, the soil underneath has eroded. Remove the eroded section and repour it. Or hire a mud-jacking company to raise the slab, inject concrete beneath it, then patch it.

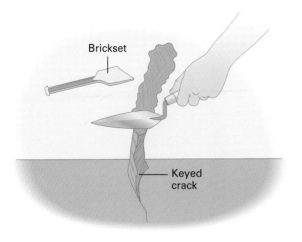

Brickset

Keyed
crack

Left: Key a crack so that the bottom is wider than the top. Wash away all dust and debris. Press vinyl patching compound into the crack, and smooth it with a trowel.

Masonry blade

to the slab's life. The patch may stand out because of its different color. If you don't like the appearance of the repair, you can resurface the area (*see page 87*).

If you have large areas that are buckling or sagging, consider hiring a mud-jacking contractor, who can raise and resupport slabs.

SMALL REPAIRS

To repair a crack in a slab, first chisel out a key. (A brickset gets the job done quickly.) Thoroughly clean away all loose material with a wire brush, and wash away dust using a scrub brush and water.

If the crack is wider than an inch, fill it with sand to about ½ inch below its surface. Wet the sand; then, using a paintbrush, work latex concrete-bonding agent into the crack. (Coat the key, don't fill it.) Allow the agent to dry.

Vinyl concrete-patching compound consists of two parts. Combine them, then fill the crack, using a pointing trowel. Push the patching compound in with the flat side of the trowel, and poke it with the tip to eliminate bubbles. Smooth the patch, first with the trowel, then with a brush.

To prepare an area of popped or spalling concrete, use a circular saw equipped with a masonry blade to key-cut the surrounding area. Chip away the interior of the area so that the recess is at least ½ inch deep at all points. Remove dust and debris, and brush on a coating of acrylic bonding agent. For small holes, use vinyl concrete-patching compound.

For a larger area, combine sand-mix concrete (which has no rocks in it) with extra portland cement (about two shovelfuls of cement per 60-pound sack of sand mix). Trowel the mixture in place, smooth and feather it with a magnesium float, and then finish it to match the surrounding concrete (*see pages 36–37*).

CONCRETE-REPAIR CAULK FOR SMALL CRACKS

Here's a simple though not permanent fix for small cracks. Clean out the crack thoroughly, using a wire brush to remove all loose matter. Fill the crack with latex caulk, making sure that it penetrates deeply. Wipe the excess with a damp rag to feather the caulk and to keep water from entering the crack. You may need to recaulk or add more caulk twice a year or so.

Above: To patch a large area, create a keyed recess using a circular saw with a masonry blade. Set the blade at a 15-degree angle and cut around the damaged area. You may need to use several passes of the saw, with the blade set slightly lower each time. Chisel away the damaged concrete.

REPAIRING STEPS

Even well-built and adequately reinforced concrete steps can suffer damage, especially at corners, at edges, and where railings are attached.

REPLACE A CHIP: If a piece that has broken off a corner or edge is salvageable, gluing it back with epoxy cement may prove to be a permanent—and desirable—repair. The replaced chip will be less apparent than a patch because it is the same color.

Using a brush and water, clean both the chip and the broken surface thoroughly but carefully so they do not crumble. Dry-fit the piece to make sure rough edges match. Mix the two parts of epoxy cement together, then apply it in a thin layer to both surfaces. Firmly press the chip into place, and wipe away excess epoxy with a rag soaked in mineral spirits.

FORM A CORNER: If you don't have a chip that fits, form the damaged area into a key that is at least ½ inch deep at all points. Use a hammer and chisel or a circular saw with a masonry blade. Brush away all loose material, and clean the area with water. Paint the keyed surface with latex concrete-bonding agent and let it dry.

Make a form with a piece of plywood. Its top should be level with the top of the step. Hold the form in place with a heavy object, such as a cement block. Mix patching cement and fill the hole, pressing down to squeeze out air bubbles. As soon as the patch hardens— which may take only a few minutes— remove the plywood and finish the edges.

FILL A HOLE: For a hole that is not at a corner, chisel out a key, and clean off debris. Apply a stiff batch of patching concrete, and use a trowel to stuff it into the hole and finish the surface.

To reattach a loose anchor bolt for a railing, chip the area around it and remove the old bolt. Deepen and widen the hole with a drill equipped with a masonry bit. Make a cardboard template of the bolt pattern; use it to position the new bolt in the hole. Test to make sure the bolt will stick out enough to anchor the railing. Mix anchoring cement or epoxy putty and pack it firmly around the bolt so it's level with the surrounding area. Check that the bolt is plumb.

Paint both the chip and the hole with epoxy cement, then press the chip into place.

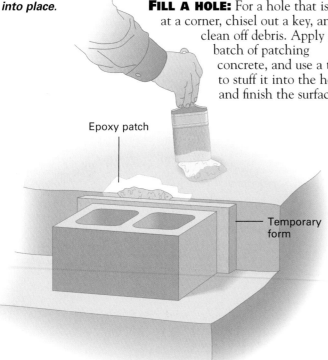

Epoxy patch

Temporary form

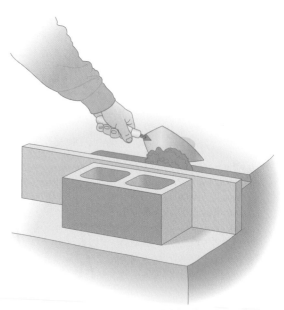

Patching concrete sets up quickly. Remove the plywood form as soon as possible to finish the patch and to smooth the edges to match the surrounding area.

RESURFACING CONCRETE

Resurfacing concrete is an intermediate repair, more substantial than patching but easier than tearing out the damaged concrete and repouring. Use this technique only if the damaged concrete is strong. Resurfacing will not glue together chunks of broken concrete.

Along each side of the area to be resurfaced, remove a few inches of sod to make room for staked forms. Install 2×4 forms so they are at least an inch above the existing concrete surface and level with each other. Every few feet, drive 2×4 stakes slightly below the top of the forms, and attach them to the forms with 3-inch deck screws.

The new control joints should be directly above the old ones, so mark the top of the forms at their positions. Use a paint roller to apply a layer of latex concrete-bonding agent to the entire concrete surface.

Mix a batch of stiff and extra-strong concrete. Add two shovelfuls of portland cement to each 60-pound bag of sand-mix concrete. Or mix your own, using 1 shovelful of portland cement to 4 shovelfuls of sand (see page 24). Add just enough water that the mix is completely wet but doesn't flow.

Shovel the concrete inside the forms, smacking it with the shovel to ensure a strong bond and to force out air bubbles. Then use a piece of 2×8 that spans the forms to pack the concrete mix, making sure the new surface is firmly pressed onto the existing concrete and eliminating air bubbles next to the forms.

Screed the area with a straight 2×4 (see pages 34–35), then float it with a wood or magnesium float. Tool with an edger and a jointer, then with a steel trowel (see pages 36–37). Finish with a broom, if you like.

Cover the new concrete with plastic or periodically spray it with water to keep it moist for a week or so.

STEPS TO RESURFACING CONCRETE

Roller-applied bonding agent

Damaged walk

1. Set the 2×4 forms at least an inch above the existing surface. Apply a latex concrete-bonding agent to the existing slab.

2. After placing the concrete and smacking it with the back of a shovel to squeeze out air bubbles, press the concrete down with a 2×8. This ensures a bond with the old surface.

Jointer trowel

When cutting control joints, position the guide directly above old joint.

3. Float, edge, joint, and finish the new surface as you would any concrete slab.

CHIMNEY REPAIRS

Far right: To clean a flue, first seal off the fireplace completely. Insert a flue-cleaning brush down into the flue, and move it up and down to dislodge debris and soot. Add brush extensions and repeat until the entire flue is clean.

Chimneys merit special attention. They are exposed to the weather, meaning that they need tuckpointing often; and they can easily deteriorate to the point where they are ready to collapse. Dirty chimneys can burst into flames. Because chimney fires are so dangerous, never light a fire in a fireplace unless you are sure the flue is clean. Follow the inspection recommendations listed below, and hire a pro whenever you aren't sure that the chimney is safe.

CHIMNEY CLEANING

Creosote, a highly flammable, tarlike substance, can collect in the flue slowly or quickly, depending on the type of wood and other materials you burn in the fireplace. If the creosote is hard and firmly stuck to the flue, call a chimney sweep to remove it. If it is flaky, you can clean it yourself, but be aware: It is messy work.

Wear a dust mask and safety goggles. Open the damper, and thoroughly seal off the fireplace with cardboard or sheets of plastic. Make the seal tight; the chunks falling down can be substantial.

Use a flue-cleaning brush that is the correct size for your flue and enough extension rods to reach the bottom of the flue. Find a stable, comfortable place to stand on the roof. Work the brush through the flue, using hard up-and-down motions. Add extension rods as needed.

When you've reamed out the entire flue, let the dust settle for an hour or so. Then carefully open the fireplace and remove the debris with a shop vacuum.

FLUE REPAIRS

If a flue is cracked, it must be relined; the bricks encasing it are not enough to shield the house from the heat of a fire. Repairing flues is a job for professionals.

In most cases, they will remove the existing flue and reline it in one of two ways. The most common is to insert a new metal liner in the chimney, then pour lightweight insulating concrete around it. They may also stuff a long vinyl balloon in the chimney, inflate it, then pour lightweight concrete around it. Once the concrete is set, they deflate the balloon and remove it.

Before hiring professionals to reline your flue, be sure they are in compliance with local codes and are bonded. Ask for a written guarantee of their work.

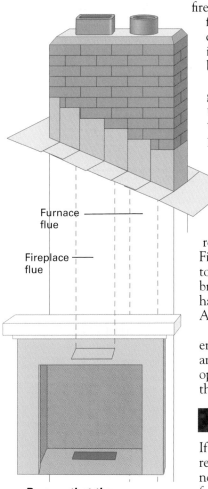

Be sure that the chimney damper can open and close completely and that the flues are free of creosote.

Furnace flue

Fireplace flue

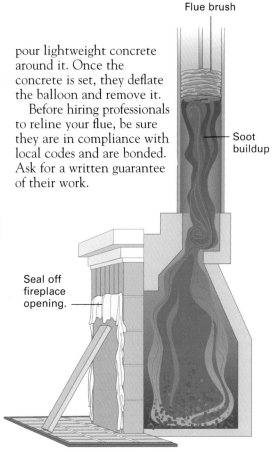

Flue brush

Soot buildup

Seal off fireplace opening.

REGULAR INSPECTION

At least once a year, take an hour or so to check the following. If you do not feel qualified to inspect it yourself, call in a pro.

■ Stabilize yourself on the roof or use binoculars from the ground, and examine the bricks and the mortar. Tuckpoint joints and replace bricks as soon as possible because loose masonry can quickly grow worse.

■ With a flashlight, examine the inside of the flue. If you see more than $1/4$ inch of flaky, crusted, or powdery matter, clean it or call in a chimney sweep before lighting a fire. If the liner looks cracked, call in a pro.

■ Open your ash pit and clean it out.

■ Make sure no branches are within 10 feet of the chimney; they can easily catch on fire. Trim them before starting a fire.

■ Check that the damper works smoothly.

■ Light a small, smoky fire to check the draw. Smoke should be drawn up readily. If not, call in a pro.

■ Look in the attic to ensure that water isn't leaking in around the chimney. If you see water stains, hire a roofer to fix the flashing—often a complicated job.

CHIMNEY CAPS

If a chimney cap is cracked, water seeping in can quickly cause considerable damage. You can simply patch small cracks, but if the old cap is crumbling, install a new one.

REPAIRING A CAP: Chisel away all loose mortar and concrete, taking care not to damage the flue. Mix some stiff mortar, adding two shovelfuls of portland cement to a 60-pound bag of mortar mix. Fill the damaged area with the mortar, and use a wood or magnesium float to smooth it. Be sure it slopes down toward the roof so water runs off.

MAKING A NEW CAP: To make a new chimney cap, build a form the same size as the old cap. Use ¾-inch plywood, and attach all the parts with screws. The inside box should be about an inch taller than the outside, to produce a slope. Attach 1×2s, see upper right, to make a drip edge, which prevents water from creeping under the cap and back to the chimney. Fill the forms with a mixture made by adding a couple of shovelfuls of portland cement to each 60-pound bag of mortar mix. Fill the form, then level it with a magnesium or wood float. After two or three days, pry the plywood pieces away from the cap. Remove the old cap from the chimney. Clean the top of the chimney, removing any debris so that it is perfectly flat. Lay a bed of mortar on the top of the chimney, and set the new cap in place. Fill the gap between the cap and the flue with patching concrete or heat-resistant caulk.

INSTALLING A WEATHER CAP

A weather cap keeps rainwater, leaves, and birds out of a chimney. In most cases, installing one takes only minutes.

Measure the outside dimensions of the flue, and purchase a weather cap to fit. Set the cap over the flue, and tighten the hold-down screws.

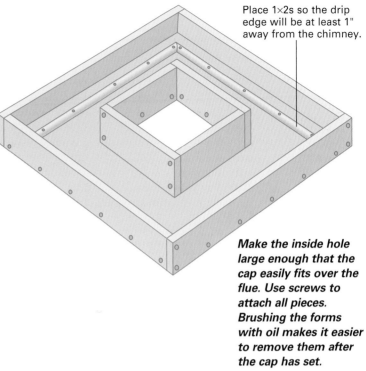

Place 1×2s so the drip edge will be at least 1" away from the chimney.

Make the inside hole large enough that the cap easily fits over the flue. Use screws to attach all pieces. Brushing the forms with oil makes it easier to remove them after the cap has set.

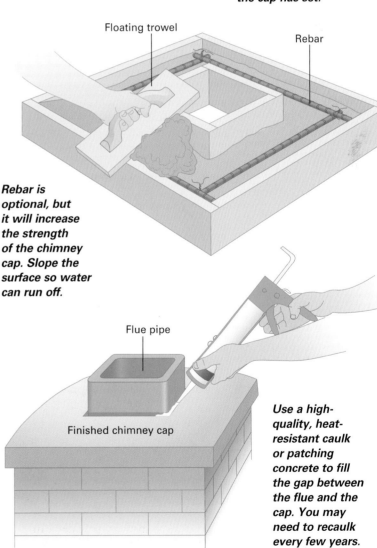

Floating trowel

Rebar

Rebar is optional, but it will increase the strength of the chimney cap. Slope the surface so water can run off.

Flue pipe

Finished chimney cap

Use a high-quality, heat-resistant caulk or patching concrete to fill the gap between the flue and the cap. You may need to recaulk every few years.

STAINS, SPALLING, AND EFFLORESCENCE

Because it is relatively soft and porous, brick is easily stained and can weaken and break down if subjected to severe weather. Check brick surfaces once a year, and take steps to protect them. The sooner you can attend to a repair, the quicker you will put a halt to damage that can spread as weather takes its toll.

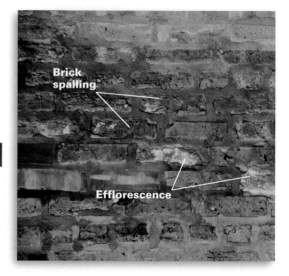

Brick spalling

Efflorescence

BRICK MAINTENANCE

A well-laid brick wall in normal weather conditions can last for a century or two without extensive maintenance. But unrepaired damage to the mortar or bricks can lead to deterioration of the wall in less than a year.

A pressure-washer often can clean efflorescence and stains from a masonry surface. Choose a fan-type nozzle. Take care not to hold it too close to the brick: The high water pressure could actually dig grooves in the bricks.

First check the mortar joints. If they allow water to seep in, serious damage to the wall can occur, especially in regions with cold winters. Tuckpoint as soon as deterioration is visible *(see pages 80–81)*.

If bricks have developed a spongy appearance, they have lost their glazed surface and are in danger of flaking apart. Apply clear masonry sealer or a couple coats of thick paint to the affected area.

If the surface of bricks are flaking off (a condition called spalling, often caused

when water seeps into the bricks and then freezes), either skim-coat the area with mortar mix or replace the individual bricks. Seal the affected area plus several surrounding bricks to prevent further spalling.

Contrary to popular belief, climbing ivy will not damage a brick wall whose mortar is in good condition. However, examine your wall in the spring before leaves appear to make sure the foliage is not hiding problems that need attention.

EFFLORESCENCE

One of the most common brick problems is efflorescence. This is a powdery white film that forms on the surface of the brick and crumbles when touched with a penknife. It results from water mixing with salts in the brick or mortar.

Recently placed mortar is particularly prone to developing efflorescence, especially if it rained while the wall was under construction. This type of efflorescence usually goes away on its own within a year.

Efflorescence on an older structure can be caused by poorly finished (or maintained) mortar joints and poor seals that allow water in around moldings and flashings. If efflorescence is found near the ground, the problem may be due to poor drainage in the soil around the foundation of the structure. Before treating the efflorescence, deal with its cause

Poultice

To improve the effectiveness of cleaning solutions, mix them with flour to make a poultice. Smear the poultice on the stain, as at left, and let it dry. As it dries, it soaks up the stain. Once dry, scrape and brush the area, then rinse with water.

Below: The best, though least attractive, way to protect a brick surface from further spalling is to cover it with a skim coat of mortar mix fortified with portland cement.

first, and make sure the wall can dry completely between rains.

To remove efflorescence, first scrub the wall thoroughly with a stiff brush, then clean the surface with a pressure-washer. Take care when using a metal brush; metal particles left behind can rust and stain the brick.

If the problem persists, wash the brick with a muriatic (hydrochloric) acid solution—1 part acid to 10 parts water. Mix carefully, and wear protective clothing. Thoroughly soak the brick with plain water. Scrub the affected area with the acid solution, then hose it off. Because the acid may change the brick color slightly, wash the surrounding area with a weaker solution to blend it.

REMOVING STAINS FROM BRICK

Stain	Treatment
Mildew	Mix 1 part bleach with 3 parts water and some laundry detergent. Use a brush to scrub the stain with this mixture, let it soak for 15 minutes, then rinse.
Old Paint	Pressure-washing may do the trick of knocking off the old paint. If not, scrape off as much paint as possible using a wire brush and putty knife. Then scrub with a mixture of trisodium phosphate (TSP) and water. If that doesn't work, use semipaste paint remover. Test first to make sure that the paint remover will not stain the brick.
Graffiti	Spray paint-remover may take off some of the graffiti. Scrape with a wire brush, or try a muriatic-acid solution. Sandblasting is a final option. To paint over graffiti, apply a stain-killing primer first.
Iron/Rust	Mix a solution of 1 pound oxalic acid with 1 gallon water, and use a brush to scrub the stain with this mixture. Let it stand for 15 minutes, then rinse thoroughly.
Smeared Mortar	Mix 1 part muriatic acid with 10 parts water, and use a wire brush to scrub the stain with this mixture. Let stand for 15 minutes, rinse, and repeat as often as necessary.
Smoke	Mix 1 part laundry detergent, 1 part bleach, and 5 parts water, then use a brush to scrub the stain with this mixture. Or, use a mixture of 1 part ammonia with 3 parts water.

REPLACING ONE BRICK OR BLOCK

If you have a few cracked or heavily spalled bricks or blocks, examine the rest of the wall to see that further damage is not imminent. Use clear sealer to protect any bricks that are starting to deteriorate.

REPLACING A BRICK: Chip out the damaged brick, using a chisel and a baby sledge. If the brick is stubborn, drill a series of holes around it with a masonry bit. Carefully chisel out the surrounding mortar so as not to damage the other bricks.

Clean and dampen the area. Lay a thick bed of mortar in the bottom of the opening; butter the top and ends of the replacement brick. Hold the brick on a board or on an upside-down brick trowel, and slide it into the opening. Strike and clean the mortar joints.

REPLACING A BLOCK FACE: It's usually not necessary to replace an entire block. Replace the face only. Drill a series of holes in the block face, and chip the face away, using a chisel and a baby sledge.

Measure the depth of the opening at several points, and mark a new block for cutting $\frac{1}{2}$ inch thinner than the opening. Cut using a circular saw with a masonry blade. Dry-set it in place to make sure it will fit. Lay a thick bed of mortar in the bottom of the opening, and butter the sides and top of the new face. Slip the face into the opening, and use wedges made from $\frac{3}{8}$-inch plywood to hold it in the center of the opening. After the mortar has become stiff, pull out the wedges and fill in the holes. Strike and clean the joints.

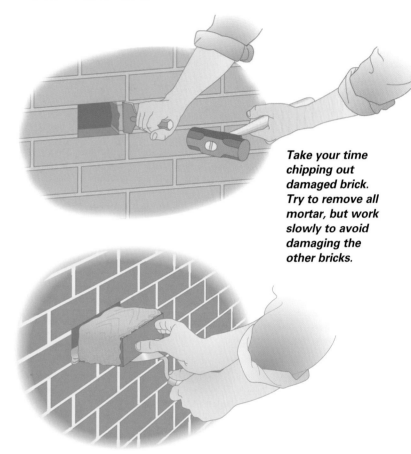

Take your time chipping out damaged brick. Try to remove all mortar, but work slowly to avoid damaging the other bricks.

Butter the top and ends of the brick and slip it onto a bed of mortar. Expect plenty of mortar to squeeze out when you shoehorn the brick into place.

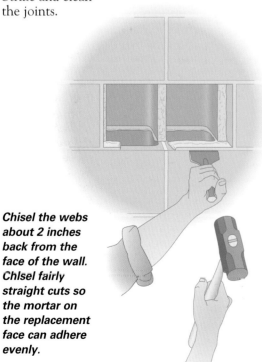

Chisel the webs about 2 inches back from the face of the wall. Chisel fairly straight cuts so the mortar on the replacement face can adhere evenly.

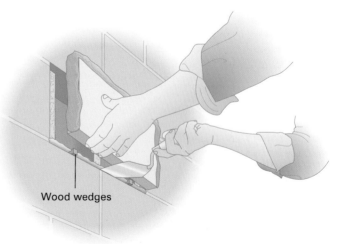

Wood wedges

Mortar alone will not center the block face in the opening, so use wood wedges. Set the face into the opening in one smooth motion; wiggling it into position may cause the mortar to lose its set. Once the mortar has set, pry out the wedges and fill the holes.

REPAIRING ASPHALT

It isn't feasible for a homeowner to lay an asphalt surface, but repairing asphalt is one of the easiest masonry jobs a homeowner can tackle.

Because asphalt (also called "blacktop") is softer than concrete, minor cracks appear in it nearly every year. Keep them from growing into major problems by coating the surface with an asphalt sealer (or "driveway sealer").

Pick a warm spring or summer day to work, when the wind is calm so leaves and debris won't be blown onto the newly coated asphalt. Wear footwear and clothing that you won't mind throwing away. It's inevitable that you'll get the sealant all over.

Trim back any grass or plants along the edge of the driveway. Sweep the driveway thoroughly, then repair cracks and any potholes. Use blacktop filler/sealer to fill holes and cracks up to ¼ inch wide. It is a bit thicker than sealer.

For a crack wider than ¼ inch, use a hammer and chisel to key it out so the bottom of the groove is wider than the top. Fill with asphalt patch, which comes in buckets or, for small jobs, in caulking tubes or plastic bottles.

If there's a large pothole in the asphalt, chisel out all the loose material and key the edges. Dig down until you reach the gravel. Add and tamp gravel to within 4 inches of the surface. Then add successive 1-inch layers of cold-mix asphalt-patching compound, tamping each successive layer. Finish by mounding the area about ½ inch above the surrounding grade. If possible, drive the wheels of a car over the patch to level it. Otherwise, tamp repeatedly. Seal the patch and the surrounding area with asphalt sealer.

When all the cracks and holes are repaired, clean the entire area with asphalt cleaner. Then apply sealer, using an inexpensive tool that looks like a push broom with a squeegee on the end. (Throw the tool away when you're done; it will be impossible to clean.) Have sawhorses or lawn chairs ready to barricade the driveway while the sealer dries.

For a small crack, use asphalt patch or driveway patch. For larger cracks, buy a bag or bucket of patching compound and apply it with a trowel.

When patching a hole, repeated tamping will make it strong. First tamp down the soil, then the gravel, then successive 1-inch layers of asphalt-patching compound.

Spread asphalt sealer with the brush side, then use the squeegee to smooth the surface. The squeegee also works well for forcing filler/sealer into cracks.

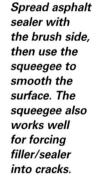

INDEX

METRIC CONVERSIONS

U.S. Units to Metric Equivalents			Metric Units to U.S. Equivalents		
To Convert From	Multiply By	To Get	To Convert From	Multiply By	To Get
Inches	25.4	Millimeters	Millimeters	0.0394	Inches
Inches	2.54	Centimeters	Centimeters	0.3937	Inches
Feet	30.48	Centimeters	Centimeters	0.0328	Feet
Feet	0.3048	Meters	Meters	3.2808	Feet
Yards	0.9144	Meters	Meters	1.0936	Yards
Square inches	6.4516	Square centimeters	Square centimeters	0.1550	Square inches
Square feet	0.0929	Square meters	Square meters	10.764	Square feet
Square yards	0.8361	Square meters	Square meters	1.1960	Square yards
Acres	0.4047	Hectares	Hectares	2.4711	Acres
Cubic inches	16.387	Cubic centimeters	Cubic centimeters	0.0610	Cubic inches
Cubic feet	0.0283	Cubic meters	Cubic meters	35.315	Cubic feet
Cubic feet	28.316	Liters	Liters	0.0353	Cubic feet
Cubic yards	0.7646	Cubic meters	Cubic meters	1.308	Cubic yards
Cubic yards	764.55	Liters	Liters	0.0013	Cubic yards

To convert from degrees Fahrenheit (F) to degrees Celsius (C), first subtract 32, then multiply by 5/9.

To convert from degrees Celsius to degrees Fahrenheit, multiply by 9/5, then add 32.

HIGH POINT PUBLIC LIBRARY
HIGH POINT, NORTH CAROLINA